THE REFERENCE SHELF (*Continued*)

Volume XX

No.

4. **Representative American Speeches: 1947-1948.** A. C. Baird. $1.50.
5. **Federal World Government.** J. E. Johnsen. $1.50.
6. **Federal Information Controls in Peacetime.** R. E. Summers. $1.50.
7. **Should the Communist Party Be Outlawed?** J. E. Johnsen. $1.50.

Volume XIX

No.

3. **Free Medical Care.** C. A. Peters. $1.25.
5. **United Nations or World Government.** J. E. Johnsen. 75c.

Volume XVIII

No.

3. **Representative American Speeches: 1944-1946.** A. C. Baird. $1.25.
5. **Anatomy of Racial Intolerance.** G. B. de Huszar. $1.25.
6. **Palestine: Jewish Homeland?** J. E. Johnsen. $1.25.

Volume XVII

No.

4. **Representative American Speeches: 1943-1944.** A. C. Baird. $1.25.
5. **Lowering the Voting Age.** J. E. Johnsen. $1.25.

Volume XVI

No.

1. **Representative American Speeches: 1941-1942.** A. C. Baird. $1.25.
2. **Plans for a Postwar World.** J. E. Johnsen. $1.25.
6. **Representative American Speeches: 1942-1943.** A. C. Baird. $1.25.
7. **Reconstituting the League of Nations.** J. E. Johnsen. $1.25.

Volume XV

No.

1. **Representative American Speeches: 1940-1941.** A. C. Baird. $1.25.
2. **Universal Military Service.** R. E. Summers and H. E. Summers. $1.25.
3. **Federal Regulation of ... Unions.** J. V. Garland. $...
7. **The Closed Shop.** J. E. Johnsen. $1.25.
9. **Permanent Price Control Policy.** J. E. Johnsen. $1.25.

...x. E. R.

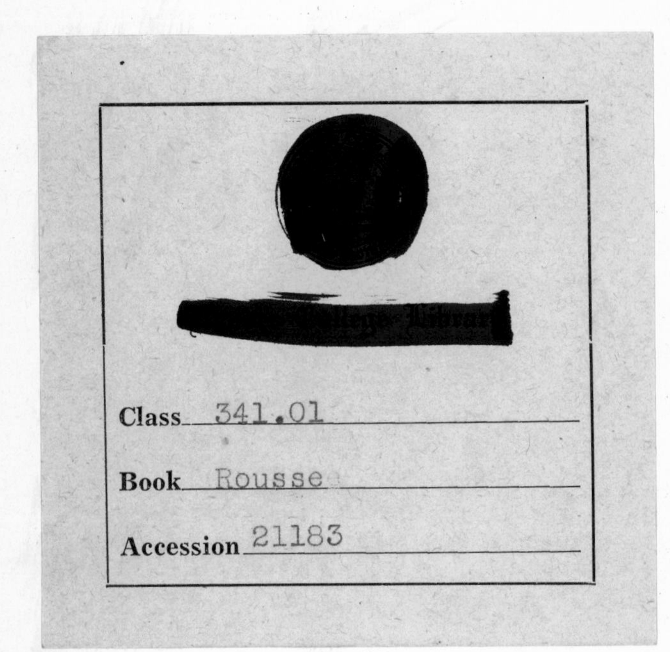

THE REFERENCE SHELF

Vol. 24 No. 1

POLITICAL ETHICS AND THE VOTER

Edited by

THOMAS A. ROUSSE

Professor of Speech, University of Texas

THE H. W. WILSON COMPANY
NEW YORK 1952

Printed in the United States of America
Library of Congress Catalog Card No. 52-6761

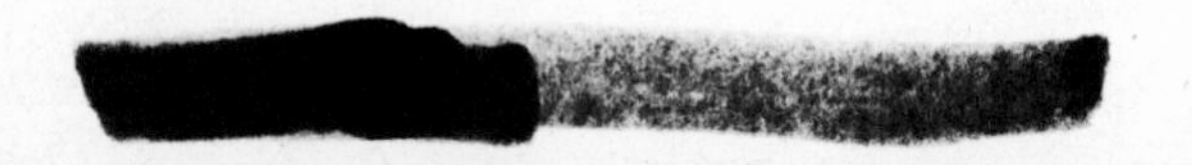

PREFACE

"Government is a trust," said Henry Clay, "and the officers of the government are trustees, and both the trust and the trustees are created for the benefit of the people." This ideal represents the hope and aspiration of all who believe in a government of, by, and for the people. The practical achievement of the democratic principles, however, has given rise to many and complex problems. This book, POLITICAL ETHICS AND THE VOTER, attempts to deal with the major problems that arise when there is a conflict between the ideal and its application in day-to-day affairs.

In the presentation of the material an attempt has been made to marshal the evidence under two main divisions: The Present Situation, and Causes and Remedies. This arrangement presents the alleged current practices at the outset of the discussion. The second division tackles the various causes and proposed remedies.

Certain assumptions, in the form of definitions, should be observed. For example, by the term *ethics* we mean the ideals and principles manifested by an individual or a people, representing a sense of values as well as standards of conduct. Consequently, *political* ethics would deal with the application of standards of conduct to elective or appointive public officials.

In order to present the various points of view and avoid excessive repetition, particularly in the section dealing with Causes and Remedies, the editor has attempted to be highly selective in the choice of articles. For the same reason, only a relatively brief list of current books and articles is included in lieu of a complete bibliography on the subject.

Grateful acknowledgment is extended to the publishers and authors for the permission to use copyright material.

THOMAS A. ROUSSE

February 1, 1952

CONTENTS

THE PRESENT SITUATION

EDITOR'S INTRODUCTION

The examination of the current practices in politics ranges from the discussion of "skullduggery" by David Lawrence to the New York *Times* sumary of the 1951 tax scandals. In addition to these the following are included: H. H. Wilson on crime and the Kefauver Committee Report; the Thomas J. Haggerty and Louise Overacker articles on the problems of campaign and political contributions; the *Guarantee Survey* contention that "big" government adversely affects moral attitudes and ethical behavior; and Gordon C. Zahn's charge that civil rights legislation is denied because of partisan politics. The last article in this section is David L. Cohn's on apathy and corruption. He registers a hopeful note, particularly where the Federal Government is concerned, when he contends that present behavior is superior to that of the past. Mr. Cohn, like Mr. Haggerty, believes that local government is the "weak" link in our political morality.

POLITICS, GOOD AND BAD[1]

Political morals seem to have taken a turn for the worse.

[1] From an editorial by David Lawrence, Editor, *United States News & World Report. United States News & World Report.* 29: 56. November 3, 1950. Reprinted by permission of *United States News & World Report,* an independent weekly magazine on national and international affairs, published at Washington, D.C. Copyright 1950, United States News Publishing Corporation.

Bad as they have been in the past, this era appears to have become tainted even more with the use of money to buy influence and special favor.

This is happening apparently on the local and state level as well as in Federal offices.

With the billions of dollars in favors which it is now possible for our governmental bodies to disburse in the form of bounties inuring to the direct advantage of special groups, can it be that the political power of the officeholder has reached unprecedented value? Is corruption to be hereafter the companion of the welfare state and of the paternalism of Federal, state and city governments?

The gamblers and the merchants of vice have always sought to buy protection from city and state authorities. Their rackets have intermittently brought on public exposure and the swift condemnation of public opinion. Courageous district attorneys have often defied gangsters and put in jail the criminals who have preyed on the people.

But money today has proved powerful enough to prevent exposures of the tie between gamblers, police and politicians in several localities. It took an action by Congress, creating the committee headed by Senator Kefauver of Tennessee, Democrat, to uncover these rackets, where millions and not just a few thousands of dollars are illegally used to prevent law enforcement. It was the action of both Republicans and Democrats in Congress which recently forced passage of the resolution of inquiry.

Federal jurisdiction touches vaguely these local situations, but the publicity given by congressional investigations will arouse the people at the state and local levels and compel the adoption of remedial measures.

The evidence thus far uncovered shows that many a large campaign contribution has been coming from racketeers into the coffers of both the national political parties. The probabilities are that the national managers knew nothing of the sources of the funds.

There is always, of course, much opportunity for corruption in the handling of campaign contributions. The Federal laws are restrictive, but the skullduggery arises when the sums gathered locally and contributed to state committees are mingled in the totals with national funds, so that the Federal inquisitors are prevented from ascertaining who really are the contributors behind the scenes.

Aside from the potentiality of evil in campaign contributions, what shall we say of the political morals of those federal officeholders who use public funds and federal employees to distribute political propaganda?

What shall we say of the political morals of an administration that in 1936 sought to garner votes from those on relief or those engaged on WPA projects?

What shall we say of the political morals of a president who in the 1930's accepted from a labor organization a $500,000 loan which was subsequently confessed by the labor leader who loaned the funds of his union to have been a purchase of governmental favor?

What shall we say of the political morals of a president who appoints to the important post of Secretary of Defense the man who collected more than $1.5 million in campaign funds for him in 1948?

What shall we say of the political morals of a president who, in order to win a municipal and state election of his political party, in 1950 uses a United States ambassadorship as a pawn in a political chess game?

What shall we say of the political morals of a governor of New York who in 1950 promises an appointive state job to a candidate if defeated?

Whether it is improper for any citizen to help a public man to pay off his personal debts in order to enable him to engage in public service—as happened when Franklin Roosevelt in 1932 and Joe Hanley in 1950 were thus aided so that they could run for office in New York State—is a question on which there will be much debate, much emotion and much prejudice. Is it unethical for a citizen to lend money to help another citizen become a candidate but ethical to give even greater sums in campaign contributions to help him get elected after he is chosen as a candidate?

The very exposure of such things may prove salutary in future appraisals.

What we need is a regeneration all along the line—a different attitude toward public service and toward politics itself.

Integrity on the part of candidates—good politics—far outweighs, however, the shocking instances of evil. As contrasted with the wrongdoers, many men and women are elected to political office regularly on the national, state and local levels in less noticed campaigns who get there through honest debate and through honorable methods, not in the slightest degree tainted with corruption. It is important that the number of such candidates for office shall increase. This can be assured only if there is a vigilant press and a vigilant public opinion.

THE PRESSURE TO BUY AND CORRUPT [2]

In January 1950, Senator Estes Kefauver introduced a bill calling for a full-scale Senate investigation of crime in interstate commerce. After a hard struggle, first with those who sought to prevent such an investigation and then to see who would control it, Kefauver and his supporters, in May 1950, succeeded in bringing into being the Special Committee to Investigate Organized Crime in Interstate Commerce.

For citizens desirous of having a permanent record of the committee's findings and recommendations, the third interim report has been made available by two private publishers, and Senator Kefauver has prepared a useful summary of the coat-to-coast hearings in his *Crime in America.* There is not, regrettably, in either his book or the committee report any significant analysis of the mass of facts, and there is little indication that either the Senators or their staff understood the implications of the material gathered.

While the hearings had vast entertainment value for newspaper readers and for the reported twenty million to thirty million television audience, it is doubtful that they contributed greatly to our understanding of the nature and sources of crime in American society or to our prospects for eliminating organized criminal activity. Only if the committee's findings are looked upon as a starting point, as a bringing up to date of one phase of the problem, will the $265,000 spent on the investigation during the first twelve months produce an adequate return.

[2] From an article by H. H. Wilson, Department of Politics, Princeton University; author of *Congress: Corruption and Compromise. Nation.* 173:45-8. July 21, 1951. Reprinted by permission.

The statements of committee members reveal curiously naïve assumptions about American society and the sources of deviant behavior. For example: that little was hitherto known of the extent of crime and political corruption; that the majority of citizens object to gambling, political favoritism, and the "fix"; that when aware of existing conditions people demand corrective reforms; that most antisocial behavior stems from the foreign-born and underprivileged; that personal pathologies are responsible for aberrant conduct; or that, as Senator Hunt observed, corruption exists "because the human heart is despicable and wicked in all things in its normal state." These assumptions are an inadequate framework for analysis of phenomena so widespread and also prevent the raising of various crucial questions. It would have been more productive, for example, to have tested the hypothesis that aberrant behavior is a symptom of conflict between culturally approved goals and narrowing opportunity for their achievement.

With no intention of belittling the sincere efforts of Senator Kefauver and his colleagues, it needs to be emphasized that the mere accumulation of additional evidence has little basic significance. Few adult citizens will be as astonished as Senator Tobey seems to have been by the committee's general conclusions: that "organized criminal gangs operating in interstate commerce are firmly intrenched in our large cities in the operation of many gambling enterprises"; that in some cities "law-enforcement officials aided and protected gangsters and racketeers"; that "there is a sinister criminal organization known as the Mafia operating throughout the country"; that "the leading hoodlums in the country remain for the most part immune from prosecution and punishment"; that the "fix" may come about through tie-ups with political machines or apparently respectable businessmen, or through corruption of the public by charitable contributions and press relations; that "the backbone of the wire service which provides gambling information to bookmakers is the leased wires of the Western Union Telegraph Company"; that "legitimate businessmen have aided the interests of the underworld by awarding lucrative contracts to gangsters and mobsters in return for help in handling employees, defeating attempts at organization, and breaking strikes." Such facts have been repeatedly documented by scores of able newspapermen from Lincoln Steffens' day to this, as well as by such investigations as those of the Chicago Vice Commission, 1911, the Senate subcommittee on "so-called rackets," 1933, or the La Follette committee, 1938.

Twenty years ago in a report written for the Wickersham Commission, Morris Ploscowe emphasized the need for fundamental social analysis:

> It is in considering the social, economic, and political factors in crime causation that one is frequently confronted with the fact that the things which are considered as contributing to crime are merely the effects of larger and more fundamental causes. To explore these causes adequately demands a thoroughgoing examination of the criminal situation in the light of the social, political, and economic development of the country. This kind of examination has unfortunately not been made, and one can merely speculate upon the effect upon crime of urban concentration, an industrial and acquisitive civilization, multiplication of contacts through rapid communication and transportation, the apparent inefficacy of democratic government to cope with modern problems, a long tradition of lawlessness, a long history of violence, etc. Though it is extremely difficult to make this kind of an examination, it is essential that it be done, so that a program of crime prevention can aim at fundamental causes and not at effects.

Despite the fact that Judge Ploscowe, now executive director of the American Bar Association's Commission on Organized Crime, worked with the Kefauver staff in preparing its final report, there is no evidence that the current Senate committee profited either by his advice or by the work of previous federal, state, and local crime studies. Similarly there is no evidence that use was made of such trenchant analyses as Edwin Sutherland's *White Collar Crime,* Thorsten Sellin's *Culture Conflict and Crime,* Lawrence K. Frank's *Society as the Patient,* or Robert K. Merton's [essay] "Social Structure and Anomie."

Apparently emotional fervor and moral uplift got in the way of realistic appraisal of crime and delinquent conduct as an integral aspect of American society. In the words of Senator Kefauver, "Serving on the Crime Committee was a tremendous emotional experience for all of us"; "emotional uplift came in the way that people from everywhere spoke of their approval of what we were trying to do"; and after the New York hearings, "my personal feelings were at a pitch of high moral indignation." It might have been more useful had the committee members remembered that people's indignation at antisocial or aberrant conduct, whether of private individuals or government officials, is rarely translated into positive action. Moral indignation may even serve as a convenient release for tensions and frustrations and, combined with our limited span of attention, provide a substitute for creative reform. As Frank has written, the "assumption of individual depravity or perversity gives us a comfortable feeling that all is well socially, but that certain individuals are outrageously violating the laws and customs that all decent people uphold."

In any case, in all the list of committee recommendations not one seems capable of rallying sustained public support or of providing opportunity for positive action. True, among its accomplishments the Crime Committee does cite the "tremendous response in the nature of public awakening and its constructive reaction to enlightenment . . . a far-reaching chain reaction" which is being expressed in grand-jury activity and "little Kefauver committees" in "many state legislatures." And it believes it "reasonable to forecast that venal politicians whose corruption has permitted the racketeers to become so firmly intrenched will in large measure be eliminated as aroused and awakened citizens go to the polls." A look at the record, however, arouses acute skepticism on this score. The history of almost any American city would show that "aroused and awakened citizens" seldom pursue reform for very long and almost never tackle the root sources of corruption. That Philadelphia has been corruptly governed for almost two generations is surely no secret to its inhabitants; James Michael Curley seems never to have been utterly repudiated by the citizens of Boston; even after the Kefauver investigation there is no obvious evidence of popular demand for the recall of Ambassador O'Dwyer; and if the people's representatives in Congress have demanded the resignation of the convicted Walter E. Brehm it has not come to notice. Nor has Congress displayed undue enthusiasm for prompt action on the legislative proposals of the Kefauver committee.

Evidence is also lacking for the committee's Jeffersonian tendency to believe that virtue resides in the small towns and rural areas. The hearings brought out that in the small towns of LaSalle and Streator, Illinois, gambler Thomas J. Cawley had been operating horse books, punchboards, baseball pools, roulette, and poker games for twenty-five years without apparent opposition from a majority of the citizens. And black-marketeer David Lubben had no difficulty in buying "a vast quantity of corn syrup in the Midwest by making under-the-table black-market payments to farmers."

"Political corruption," according to Lincoln Steffens, "is not a matter of men or classes or education or character of any sort; it is a matter of pressure. Wherever the pressure is brought to bear, society and government cave in. The problem, then, is one of dealing with the pressure, of discovering and dealing with the cause or the source of the pressure to buy and corrupt." We need to know what it is in society that forces individuals to pursue socially defined and approved goals by unlawful means. We have reached a stage in our national development where the exclusive pursuit of individual ends may well cause the disintegration of our society. It is not enough for the committee to say that success in the fight against crime and corruption "depends on the uplifting of standards of public and private morality, a rededication to basic spiritual values which will entail righteous indignation over" these conditions. Nor does Spruille Braden's suggestion—"I sometimes wonder if the Soviet is not, at least in some measure, inciting these vermin to defile our system of law and order"—advance our understanding. Let's face it: graft, crime, corruption, the "fix" are imbedded in the very fabric of our highly competitive society.

The closest Senator Kefauver comes to discussing this basic problem is when he writes: "In many big cities young people come to maturity with an attitude of contempt for law, because they see and hear almost daily of instances wherein criminals, through alliances with conniving politicians and crooked law-enforcement officers, are bigger than the law." He might usefully have gone on to discuss the impact on young people of the employment by the Phelps-Dodge Copper Products Company of gangster Anthony Anastasia (an incident which he does not treat in *Crime in America*), or of the Ford Motors Company's contract with Joe Adonis, or of the relations of the Detroit Stove Works and the Briggs Manufacturing Company with gangsters.

A certain naïveté marks the report's treatment of business tie-ups with the underworld. We are told that "in fairness to Ford Motor Company it should be noted that it is taking vigorous steps to disassociate itself from these racketeer-held contracts." Apparently we are to assume that this represents revulsion from newly discovered contamination, although at least one of the contracts had existed for twenty years! At any rate we should be thankful that "Ford has publicly deplored this situation." In general it is puzzling that the Crime Committee should be so sanguine about the possibility of raising standards of public and private morality when the hearings reveal that business élites are not receptive to this rededication. "Practically every large distillery and brewery has granted franchises to racketeer dealers," but "they were almost all vague on the question of whether they would fire a distributor upon finding he had criminal associations." Similarly, though Senator Kefauver was irritated by California's "million-dollar lobbyist," Arthur H. Samish, he failed to develop the implications of the fact that Schenley Distillers of New York paid Samish $36,000 a year, or that the California State Brewers' Institute provided him with another $30,000 salary, "plus control of a $153,000-a-year slush fund."

The record of business during World War II suggests that even patriotism is inadequate to overcome other pressures operating in our society. The Senate National Defense Committee had no difficulty in compiling a list of major firms wiling to take advantage of the national crisis, and Marshall Clinard has reported that at least 11 per cent of all retail firms violated OPA regulations in 1944. As a matter of fact, the million OPA violations in one year practically equaled the number of all other crimes known to the police in the same period. Though we do not place these white-collar criminals in the same category with violators of other laws, the financial loss from white-collar crime is probably greater than that from all other crimes combined. As Edwin Sutherland has demonstrated, its impact on our institutions and morale is infinitely greater.

The white-collar criminals resist efforts to enforce the criminal law against themselves by attacks, through the agencies of public opinion which they control, on the integrity of public officials and private parties who object to white-collar crime. These attacks result in further disintegration of the society.

Of the twenty-two recommendations of the Kefauver committee, one could be tremendously valuable—the creation of a Federal Crime Commission one of whose functions would be "the initiation and development of appropriate social study relating to crime, its punishment, and law enforcement." What is needed is a detailed analytical study of American society, its premises, values, institutions, and the forces operating to produce social disorganization and anomie. The findings of the Kefauver committee should be combined with those of the New York narcotics investigation, the Fulbright study of the Reconstruction Finance Corporation, the "five per-centers" material, the studies of businessmen and the black market, relevant sections of the Truman committee findings, even the results of the Douglas committee on ethics and the Delaney committee on the use of chemicals in foodstuffs. Until the American public understands that these are all facets of the same problem—social disorganization, the disintegration of a traditional culture, the absence of common individual or social ends—investigations will do little more than compound the popular cynicism.

The narrow investigation of crime as the violation of law must be broadened to include the concept of delinquency—"those forms of behavior disorder which manifest themselves in injury to others or to society"—and the whole area of white-collar crime. That 350 unmarked trucks a month have been detected trying to enter the Holland and Lincoln tunnels carrying explosives or inflammable loads since the serious explosion in the Holland Tunnel in 1949 is more revealing of the general social malaise than is some individual's activity in betting on sporting events. The needed study of social morale would be aided by a comparative analysis of conditions in another society. A team of social scientists might therefore be sent to Great Britain, where some evidence suggests that deviant behavior is less common and that conflict between socially approved goals and means has been less acute. It would be a difficult assignment, for no culture can be realistically analyzed without a searching examination of its basic premises, institutions, and sacred idols—or without stepping on the toes of the righteous and the wielders of power. If this is too big or too delicate a task for the United States Congress, perhaps one of the foundations could be persuaded to do it.

SPOILS AND THE RACKET [3]

Never since I have been able to read and comprehend a political party platform have I failed to see the word "economy" included in its make-up as one of the cardinal planks. To fail to mention it would be considered a grave oversight on the part of the political boss.

Notwithstanding this fact, I have, except on one or two occasions, failed to see it materialize in a way that the word would imply. The reason for this, it seems to me, needs to be explained to one not versed in practical politics.

In this country, candidates for public office are generally elected through the efforts of a political party or machine, which undertakes to sell the candidate to the electorate of the particular district he desires to represent. Now, in order to conduct this campaign, organization, workers, and money are required. If the party under whose banner the candidate is campaigning happens to be in power in that particular district, the sailing is not so rough. Should it not be in power, the going is quite choppy. . . .

Plus organization and workers, a campaign requires money. To the party in power this need not prove a great obstacle. To the "outs" it is a real problem. To the campaign fund of the "ins," every illegitimate business or racket contributes, along with some that are strictly legitimate. The head of the illegitimate business contributes because he cannot do otherwise. If he is operating under the present regime, he is perfectly satisfied anyway and wants no change. The legitimate busi-

[3] From an article by Thomas J. Haggerty, a businessman active in municipal politics in New York and New Jersey. *Annals of the American Academy of Political and Social Science.* 189:17-21. January 1937. Reprinted by permission.

ness contributes sometimes to both sides. It is good policy to be on friendly terms with those that are in and to be in the good graces of the outs should they become ins. This may sound strange, but nevertheless it is a fact.

If the party in power elects its ticket, things shortly quiet down; the boss surveys the field, sees who performed well, and, if they are not already on the pad or payroll, creates jobs for them.

Should the outs become the ins, the story is slightly different. The first thing they do is to sweep out of office every trace of the former regime and set about to install a brand new regime of faithful party workers. The number of jobs given out is usually larger than before, because the newly elected party campaigned on limited cash supplemented by a sea of promises of jobs "if we go over." So, almost any day after the newcomers take office, you will find them besieged by an army of job seekers, a great many of whom will be placed on the pad.

Now, when does this promise of economy go into effect? It just doesn't. The promise is merely part of the game. The new ins have been out so long that they are like a pack of hungry wolves. . . .

Installed in office, this new administration sets out to do just what the previous one of another party did, namely, dispense favor and patronage and collect tribute. In short, it concentrates on building an organization or machine in order to perpetuate itself in power. This is accomplished in a variety of ways.

In some states, judges are elected to office in the same way as any other candidate. Their names must be placed on the ballot to be voted upon. But the fact that the aspirant for the judgeship has every qualification for the position is not enough. He must be strictly organization; he must obey orders. . . .

The racketeer, of which there are several kinds, plays more than a small part in machine politics. The fellow who runs a handbook, the betting commissioner, the labor leader racketeer, the fellow who furnishes protection and collects from establishments of ill fame, all look to the powers that be to carry on. No racket could operate longer than seventy-two hours without the O.K. . . .

The ins collect from various sources such as I have outlined above. Do you suppose for a moment that the outs do not know where these sources of tribute are located? They certainly do, or they would not be boss politicians. So the ins see that the outs get a percentage of the shakedown in order to keep the outs from letting out a cry about graft.

Of course, the outs do not get anything like the share the ins retain for themselves. Furthermore, the outs share in the racketeering graft only. The cut on purchase of school supplies, fuel, or new buildings, or alterations of old ones, which goes to the ins, is retained in its entirety. This is not generally known. Even the run-of-the-mill members usually do not know about it.

While on this phase of the subject, let us look into the affair a little farther. The party that is out locally may be in power in either the Federal or the state government or both, and from this source the local outs may, and probably will, be able to get some pap. Of course, national and state pap is not nearly so plentiful as local pap, unless you include the WPA ("With Political Approval"). . . . The local ins may, and usually do, have to curry favors which have to do with state or national affairs. Being of a different party from the ins in the nation or the state, they cannot contact or make the connection. The chairman of the city committee of the local outs has the approach for any pap or favors when his party is in power in the state or the national government. It must come through him. This gives the local outs a chance for a cut and also an opportunity to build up a machine. Despite the fact that the local ins have a representative in the state or national body, Mr. Chairman of the local outs or one of his henchmen is the one who will handle the matter if the body as a whole is predominantly of another or opposing party.

We come to positions under Civil Service. These positions are supposed to be filled by those who have passed an examination with highest ratings. But are they? Invariably you will find a person far down on the list being appointed to a position while someone with a much higher rating looks on in bewilderment. The one less qualified more likely than not has the connection, plus cash to the amount of the first year's salary. Suppose he has the connection but not the cash? Well, what is the Morris plan for? Promissory notes and endorsers are still recognized by banks, and what a volume of business banks do along these lines!

About four weeks ago I read in a New York daily paper a statement by a high official of the Civil Service who spoke about the pressure brought on him from time to time to favor certain people on various lists when making appointments. He said that usually a person interceding for someone else was of the professional class —a clergyman, a lawyer, a physician, a certified public accountant. Investigation proved that in a great many cases the individual did not even know the applicant in whose behalf he was speaking. This is not strange, but it does seem that a person who has had the advantage or benefit of a good education should be using it for a better purpose.

The political boss gets his power from the ballot box, the actual results of which are sometimes questionable. Be that as it may, his organization gets out the vote. Into the polling place come people of every mental capacity, from the scholar, the real intellectual who has absorbed the untranslated works of Virgil, Theocritus, Plato, and Horace and has delved into problems in fourth dimensional geometry, to the dodo who hardly knows how to spell his own name, to say nothing of knowing what the election is all about. The workers who get out the vote ignore the scholar, who exists in very limited numbers, but devote all, or nearly all, their time to the dodo who, in numbers, constitutes the mob. Those voters do not vote, but are voted the way the boss says; sometimes for pay, sometimes for favors to come. The result is usually referred to as the mob vote. . . .

Boss rule in politics has made the game (and indeed it is a game) so vicious, so brutal, that sensitive and delicate persons remain aloof from it. Those who might be a real asset to public life recoil farthest from it. . . .

Contrary to what many people may think, the mainstays of the political machine are not in Washington, D.C., or in the state legislature, but are back in the home precincts where the heelers get out the vote. Collectively, these districts spell victory or defeat. Usually, the closer is the candidate to the electorate, the poorer the choice. State government is less efficiently administered than your national government, and your cities are less efficiently administered than your state government. . . .

This is not the most pleasant side of public life about which to write. But this phase of it prevails, so much that it seriously threatens to become bigger than government itself. It has, to no small degree, undermined confidence in government; the man in public life is looked upon as a grafter, someone to be avoided. It has helped to form the opinion that what passes for government is just a racket, thinly disguised. This is strong language, I know, but it describes the situation better than any other word I know.

DIRTY MONEY AND DIRTY POLITICS[4]

An astute student of politics once said: "No people can be free who do not maintain the privilege of paying their own bills." Yet Americans not only are not paying their own bills, but show little interest in who does. The financing of the election campaign of 1948 has never been put under the microscope by an investigating committee, ugly rumors go the rounds in Washington about the sources from which the Democrats drew some of their support, and limitations which encourage evasion remain upon the statute books. . . .

We know much more about who supported the parties and the candidates in 1944 than we do about who filled our campaign chests in 1948. Following procedure consistently in use since 1912, special congressional committees in 1944 filled in many details missing from the reports required of party committees and candidates under the federal Corrupt Practices Act. The Political Action Committee of the CIO, and other non-party opinion-molders were closely studied by a House committee. A Senate committee, headed by Theodore F. Green of Rhode Island, assembled data relating to a vast number of party committees, independent organizations and candidates and made available what is probably the

[4] From an article by Louise Overacker, author of several books in the field of politics and member of the Committee on Political Parties of the American Political Science Association. *New Republic.* 123: 11-13. September 11, 1950. Reprinted by permission.

most accurate and complete picture ever recorded of the financing of elections in a presidential campaign year.

Piecing together the story of the financing of a national campaign in the United States is not easy. In addition to party and non-party political committees carrying on activities in two or more states, money may be raised and spent quite independently by a host of state, county, assembly-district and local committees. Only those committees operating on behalf of presidential candidates in two or more states are required to report regularly to Washington. In addition, candidates for the Senate and House file certain information about what they receive and spend on their final election campaigns.

Obviously, much of the story lies outside these reports. State and local committees are not covered, although what they raise and spend clearly affects the fortunes of national candidates; primary elections and elections of delegates to the nominating conventions fall outside the scope of national regulations, although they may be covered by the Corrupt Practices Acts of the respective states; some non-party organizations, whose activities may affect the fortunes of parties and candidates, do not file, claiming that their activities are educational, not political, in character. The omission of such expenses as postage, traveling and telephone service from the reports filed by candidates for the Senate and House, and of funds raised by committees and individuals operating independently of these candidates, leaves other wide gaps in our information.

With the power to go behind the record, call witnesses and use field investigators, many of these gaps can be filled in by a congressional committee. Equally important is the service such a committee can perform in fitting together pieces of a puzzle which mean nothing separately but become part of a meaningful pattern once they have found their place in the whole. Without the work of a congressional committee the far-flung activity of "wet" and "dry" groups and others in the Hoover-Smith campaign of 1928 would never have been brought to light; we would not have known, for example, that a single individual gave more than $170,000 to various anti-Smith groups. It was a Senate committee which publicized the part labor played in financing the second Roosevelt campaign. If there had been no Senate investigation of the 1944 campaign we should not have known that nine members of the Pew family contributed more than $108,000 to various Republican committees—national, state and county.

Putting together the pieces of the jigsaw puzzle is even more difficult today than it was before 1940, because of certain limitations included in the Hatch Act of that year. Piously proclaiming that "money is the chief source of corruption," Congress added amendments placing a ceiling of $5,000 upon individual contributions to a political committee and limiting to $3 million the annual expenditures of any committee operating in two or more states. Since 1940, first by the Smith-Connally Anti-Strike Act of 1943 and later by the Taft-Hartley Act of 1947, political contributions by labor organizations have been prohibited.

These limitations, without reducing expenditures, have led to an unfortunate splintering of fund-raising activities. Independent committees have mushroomed. In 1944 they spent twice as much as the Democratic National Committee and four times as much as the Republican National Committee. The $5,000 limitation upon individual contributions was circumvented with ease. Gifts could be hung on many branches of a family tree, or routed through numerous committees. Sixty members of the Du Pont clan contributed more than $200,000 to various Republican agencies in 1940. By distributing his gifts among committees scattered from the Eastern seaboard to Wyoming, one member of this family gave a total of $49,000 to the Republican campaign. Nor did the restrictions upon trade unions prevent them from playing an important part in financing the 1944 campaign. By creating Political Action Committees with independent treasuries, CIO unions and their friends invested $1.3 million in the campaign. In 1948 the AFL, through a newly created Labor's Educational and Political League, joined the CIO-PAC in raising funds to defeat candidates who had supported the Taft-Hartley Act.

Is it less pernicious for fifteen committees working for the same candidate to spend $15 million than for one to do so? Is any useful purpose served by a prohibition which transfers the expenditures of funds from the CIO or the AFL to organizations cooperating with them? . . .

Where does the money come from? Broadly, the funds for a campaign come from candidates, their personal friends, office seekers and officeholders, gamblers and other law-breakers who want protection, other special interests, and the public. The relative importance of certain sources of course varies with the time and place. Officeholders are no longer so vulnerable to compulsory assessments; underworld contributions are more important locally than nationally; the Jackson Day dinner of the Democrats is a comparatively painless device; trade unionists nowdays pay their own political bills.

An important change in financial support is reflected in the funds of the two national committees. In 1904, when Theodore Roosevelt opposed Alton B. Parker, much of the $2 million spent by the Republicans was contributed by corporations in amounts of $50,000 or more. At that time, two wealthy men gave most of the $700,000 which financed the Democratic National Committee. Following the revelation of these disturbing facts, contributions from corporations were prohibited. More important, Congress passed laws requiring national party committees to file statements of their contributions and expenditures. By 1928, participation in the financing of the campaign was considerably broader; more than 90,000 individuals contributed to the Democratic National Committee and the impressive number of 140,000 to the Republican. Less reassuring, however, was the role of the large contributor. Half of the Democratic fund was given by 135 supporters in amounts of $5,000 or more, and contributions of less than $100 accounted for only 12 per cent of the total. On the Republican side, 45 per cent of the fund came from 300 persons in amounts of $5,000 or more, and an insignificant 8 per cent of the total was contributed in amounts of $100 or less. Disturbing, also, was the fact that both parties leaned heavily upon bankers and manufacturers.

By the second Roosevelt campaign significant changes could be noted in the financing of the Democratic party. In 1936, although the National Committee received some large contributions, including one gift of $102,500 from a Pittsburgh oil man, more than one third of its funds came from small contributors in amounts of less than $100. Jackson Day dinners, sale of the "book of the Democratic Convention," commemorating that event, and contributions to a Roosevelt Nominators' Division accounted for most of it. Various labor groups, mainly CIO affiliates, gave $770,000, including $250,000 which went directly to the Democratic National Committee.

The GOP continued to draw upon traditional sources. Two families, the Du Ponts and the Pews, together gave $1,000,000 of the $7,760,000 the Republican National Committee received.

The Hatch Act, passed just as the whistle blew for the 1940 Presidential contest, encouraged the decentralization of fund-raising but did not alter the sources of financial support of the parties. Small contributors continued to rally to the Democrats, though in both 1940 and 1944 that party got some money from oil operators. The Republicans went on getting contributions from bankers, manufacturers, and wealthy families.

The high cost of campaigning goes higher and Republicans frankly appeal to the large contributor for support. Democrats encourage "peanut" contributions but are suspected of being under financial obligation to "big oil." The problem is one which existing limitations have not solved, and cannot. It is no comfort to a candidate who cannot possibly scrape together $10,000 from respectable sources, to know that his competitor is limited to $25,000. The problem is not only that some have too much, but that others have too little. "Ceilings" which encourage special interests to scatter their support far and wide among committees working for the same political ends do not alter the dependence upon those interests. They merely make it harder for Congress, the press and the public to obtain essential facts.

Existing federal regulations of campaign funds have repeatedly been branded as utterly inadequate. With few exceptions, state Corrupt Practices Acts are even less effective. It is high time we changed our attitude toward a problem which strikes at the foundations of our democratic structure, and try to work out a constructive approach. An important first step would be to exploit fully every existing means of assembling data about the financing of campaigns and to make that information available to every voter. By implementing standing committees of Congress with permanent professional staffs, the Legislative Reorganization Act of 1946 paved the way for systematic, continuous investigation of campaign funds. But in 1948 neither the Senate Committee on Rules and Administration nor the Committee on House Administration, through its respective subcommittees on privileges and elections, took advantage of this opportunity. No summary of the pertinent facts about the financing of the campaign was ever made public. The report of a special committee, headed by Representative Ross Rizley of Oklahoma, was limited to specific charges of illegal and unethical action in certain districts. When we need more publicity, we have less.

Perhaps if we were fully aware of where the campaign dollars come from, we might decide it would be cheaper to pay our own political bills. A system of party membership dues, with some of the revenue flowing back to the state and local organizations, would give the parties a more stable, explicit basis as well as a much more democratic financial support. In some other countries parties are financed largely by dues-paying memberships. If a political organization stands for objectives of real importance to its members, it ought to be worth supporting with dollars as well as with votes.

ECONOMICS AND MORALS [5]

What is happening to America's ethical standards? Thoughtful people concerned with moral issues seem to be asking this question more seriously as time brings

[5] From an editorial in *Guaranty Survey,* published monthly by the Guaranty Trust Company of New York. 41:1-4. November 1951. Reprinted by permission.

successive disclosures of shady and even criminal practices in public and private dealings. Are those disclosures accidental, or do they reflect a real moral deterioration? Is there any connection between the sale of Federal jobs and the sale of narcotics to school children? Can bribes to income-tax collectors and bribes to college basketball players be traced to some common cause or causes, other than the frailty of human nature? If so, what is the cause, and what can be done about it?

Congress also is asking these questions. A Senate subcommittee has submitted a report on "Ethical Standards in Government" which deals realistically with some aspects of the subject, although as a whole it is not so much concerned with underlying trends and causes as with legislative remedies for specific evils.

In the search for possible explanations, surprisingly little attention has been given to the socio-economic philosophy which government officials have expounded and exemplified to the people for almost twenty years. The essence of this philosophy is that the government should extend its power over economic life in the effort to achieve aims that are deemed socially desirable. Such a sweeping program is bound to have far-reaching effects on both the government and the individual citizen. Some of those effects may be well worth considering in connection with the question of public and private morality.

It is not self-evident that our moral standards actually are lower today than they have been in the past. Those who have seen the record of the Grant Administration, those who remember the cabinet scandals of the 1920's, and those who are familiar with the unsavory political history of many of our cities will not be too quick to conclude that we have sunk to a new depth of civic depravity. This much, however, does seem certain:

Wrongdoing in public office becomes more serious as the government extends its authority over the people's private affairs. The Senate's investigating subcommittee apparently believes that ethical standards have risen but that "the need for high standards of integrity . . . has grown even faster." Official conduct that is deplorable in a government of limited powers can be ruinous in a welfare state. Is it possible that the left-wing crusade which started with such battle cries as "special privilege," "monopoly," "graft," "corruption," and "social responsibility" has backfired, and that the old abuses are still with us under new forms, with the difference that now they are worse than ever, because they penetrate more deeply into the lives of the people? If a certain degree of governmental corruption is unavoidable, can the benefits that are hoped for from the welfare state be reasonably expected to outweigh its implicit evils? . . .

No phenomenon of our time . . . has more profoundly affected the nature and scope of governmental activities and the livelihoods of the people than the enlarged conception of the functions of government in economic affairs. It is strange that the possible moral implications of this plain and significant fact should have been so largely overlooked.

How does the trend toward "big government" affect moral attitudes and ethical behavior?

Most obvious, perhaps, is the fact that big government means high costs, and high costs mean high taxes. The tax burden per capita in the United States has risen from about $80 in 1927 to $360 in 1950. Tax rates on the top brackets of individual income are close to the point of complete confiscation. . . . The temptation is strong to evade taxation at such rates, and it is not to be wondered at that evasion sometimes crosses the line between the legal and the illegal. The pressure affects taxpayers and tax collectors alike.

Big government also means big spending, which brings opportunities for abuses of many kinds. Mink coats, deep freezers, and expensive vacations fall to the lot of officials, their families, and their friends. The peddling of influence by "five per-centers" becomes a profitable business. Government employees resign to take lucrative jobs with companies they have helped by loans or contracts. Public servants, having established valuable contacts with key officials, find it profitable to withdraw from government service and use those contacts as "legal advisers" to parties seeking favors from the government. Some of them even manage to keep their jobs and go into private business "on the side"—business, of course, that touches the far-flung activities of government at strategic points. Even members of Congress and military personnel, unfortunately, have not proved wholly immune to the temptations that big spending involves.

One of those who participated in the drafting of the bill creating the Reconstruction Finance Corporation recently described that institution as providing a "pipeline from the Treasury to the voter." It is only one of many such pipelines. In fact, a central government that collects and distributes annually, in peacetime, something like 16 per cent of the national income may be fairly characterized as providing a pipeline from the taxpayer to the voter. As the scale of government expenditures has risen, the nation has been brought face to face with the problem of "pressure groups" representing large blocks of votes and demanding financial benefits for their members. These groups do not regard themselves as sellers of votes but as organized minorities fighting for their "rights." But when the "rights" consist of grants from the public purse and are enforced by voting threats, they are dangerously close to the borderline of extortion.

The recipients of largess from "big government," with their families, constitute a numerous body of voters. Reinforcing them is the bureaucracy itself. Civilian Federal employees (about 90 per cent of whom live outside the District of Columbia) now number approximately 2.5 million, or more than four times as many as in 1929. With their families, relatives, and friends, they represent several times that number of votes. These two blocks of "payroll votes" combined account for a substantial proportion of the electorate. Thus "big government" creates vested interests which are far more powerful politically than any that ever existed or could have existed in the past.

The same principles apply to all exercise of governmental power, not merely that involving the collecting and spending of money. As government extends its authority over economic affairs, public decisions on specific questions become enormously important to individuals and groups. The persons who make or affect those decisions are exposed to great temptations, whether in the form of money, votes, political preferment, threats, personal obligations or attachments, or any other form of pressure. Inside knowledge of coming decisions may enable officials to enrich themselves by speculation or by selling such information to others. "All power tends to corrupt; absolute power corrupts absolutely." Those words were written more than half a century ago, but they have taken on new significance with recent tendencies in government. . . .

As the authority of government increases, the scope of individual initiative shrinks. People find that their welfare depends less on their own productive efforts and activities, and more on the decisions of bureaucrats. As their freedom of action diminishes, their sense of responsibility weakens. Their hopes center more and more on the possibility of getting something for nothing. The idea of receiving payment for services rendered tends to give way to the idea of simply receiving payment. . . .

Of all the private rights invaded by the state, none has been so hard hit as the right of ownership. When the state takes from Peter and gives to Paul it is saying, in effect, that what Peter has is not rightfully his; Paul should have it instead. One effect of such practices is to weaken the whole concept of ownership. The commandment "Thou shalt not steal" has no meaning except in relation to the right of property, for obviously it is impossible to steal what does not belong to someone else. Every doubt that is cast on the rightness of ownership is a doubt on the wrongness of stealing. May not this have something to do with the apparent prevalence of thievery, including the "alarming" increase in embezzlements reported by the Federal Bureau of Investigation and other agencies?

Not only the injunction against theft, but almost all the traditional moral standards in business dealings, presuppose a social order in which private property and private enterprise are recognized as inviolable rights: Any weakening of the rights is a blow at the moral standards based upon them. This tendency toward the breakdown of long-accepted ethical principles finds its logical fulfillment in communist ideology, in which such "bourgeois" virtues as fair dealing, truth-telling, and performance of contracts have no place. Has not the trend toward the welfare state carried us some distance in that direction? . . .

One of the favorite accusations of the new self-styled "liberals" against free private enterprise is its alleged lack of "social responsibility." Volumes could be written in answer to this charge. But what about the "social responsibility" of the "liberals" themselves? No faults or shortcomings of private enterprise can be nearly as dangerous as the misuse of power in a welfare state governed by officials whose sense of "social responsibility" fails to keep pace with their authority.

TAX SCANDALS: AN ISSUE FOR '52 [6]

The history of political corruption in America has many chapter headings—the "Whiskey Ring" with its liquor-tax evasion under Grant; the "Star Route Frauds," involving stagecoach mail contracts under Garfield; the "Teapot Dome Scandal," involving lease of government oil lands under Harding, as well as innumerable local "tin box" and "little black book" scandals.

Now there is being written a new chapter—one that could be entitled "The Mink Coat Scandals." Actually, the mink coats are a small part of the story; a few government officials got them, free or cut-rate, through businessmen with whom they had official dealings. Nevertheless, the mink coats have come to symbolize a succession of scandals in the Truman Administration. The klieg lights of Washington investigations have glared down upon an almost uninterrupted parade of "five-percenters," "influence peddlers" and "fixers." The extent of the corruption is not known, but corruption there is.

The disclosures so far have had a heavy impact upon the national consciousness. Corruption is certain to be a big issue in the elections next year. It is a rare Repub-

[6] From an article in the New York *Times*. p E1. December 9, 1951. Reprinted by permission.

lican orator nowadays who does not throw in at least a mention of "mink coats."

Last week—as in several weeks past—the theme was corruption involving taxes. A Congressional inquiry into collectors of taxes and enforcers of tax laws produced new and serious charges against high officials. There was some criticism of the inquiry itself; the Congressional investigators were accused of allowing themselves to be used as a vehicle for irresponsible accusations.

This is how tax collection and enforcement work:

Taxpayer X files his income tax return with his district Collector of Internal Revenue—there are sixty-four collectors throughout the country. If Mr. X's income is under $7,000 a year, it is—in theory—examined in the collector's office. Actually, since there are upward of 50 million returns on incomes under $7,000 and only 33,000 employees in the collectors' offices, about 7.8 per cent of the under-$7,000 returns are examined.

If Mr. X's income is over $7,000 a year, his return goes to his district Internal Revenue Agency—there are thirty-nine throughout the country. About 2.5 million tax returns are in this category. The higher the income is, the greater the chances are that the return will be examined. For example, district revenue agents examine 17.2 per cent of the returns of incomes between $10,000 and $25,000 and 86.4 per cent of the over-$100,000 returns.

If, on examination, a district revenue agent suspects that Mr. X is cheating the government, the agent brings his findings to the district Intelligence Unit — fifteen throughout the country. Revenue and Intelligence agents then investigate jointly.

If there is any evidence of tax delinquency or fraud, Mr. X's case can be categorized as a civil violation and brought before a tax court. The biggest penalty for civil cases is payment of back taxes plus 50 per cent. In the fiscal year 1950 the Justice Department received about 230 such cases.

But if the agents think they can prove beyond a reasonable doubt that Mr. X is guilty of willfully falsifying his return they can try to bring him to book for criminal fraud. The procedure is long and involved; the case must be examined and the briefs approved by the Internal Revenue Bureau's Penal Division in Washington, by the bureau's chief counsel, and by the Commissioner's office. Finally, the case goes to the Tax Division of the Department of Justice, which is charged with prosecuting criminal tax cases. The Tax Division makes its own examination and if it agrees with the Internal Revenue Bureau's findings, it sends the case to the United States attorney in Mr. X's district. Ultimately Mr. X is brought before a United States District Court and prosecuted for criminal tax delinquency. In fiscal 1950 the Justice Department closed criminal prosecutions against 710 defendants and got convictions of about 420. The maximum penalty is five years in prison and a $10,000 fine—plus back taxes. The whole process takes about three and one-half years. During that period anyone in any of the divisions along the way can make a recommendation against prosecution.

For about a year there have been reports of "irregularities" involving income tax collection and enforcement. Last September a House Ways and Means subcommittee headed by Representative Cecil R. King, California Democrat, began conducting open hearings into the situation. Out of the hearings there has emerged a shadowy picture of government employees who accepted favors from taxpayers under investigation, of cases against businessmen who "knew someone" being dropped, of zealous agents being transferred to other departments.

Meanwhile, the Administration has been conducting its own investigation into the tax situation. The President and the Treasury Department have already fired some fifty important tax officials, some of whom face prosecution. The Internal Revenue Bureau and the Justice Department are preparing cases against others. Government employees dealing with tax matters are jittery. Many, leery of making decisions that might be challenged, are passing the buck on questionable tax returns to their superiors. In one instance a reporter, asking an Internal Revenue man about procedure, said, "Now, suppose I filed my tax return at your office—" He interrupted, saying "Listen, if you filed your return at my office I won't talk to you about it."

When the current phase of the investigation ends, the King subcommittee still will have much work ahead. . . .

Accordingly tax scandals are likely to be in the headlines right down to the beginning of next year's presidential campaign. The consensus is that the corruption issue will hurt the Administration politically.

CIVIL RIGHTS AND POLITICAL INTEGRITY [7]

The success of a two-party system depends to a large extent upon party responsibility and accountability. This can be achieved only if the individual party members accept their obligation to use the powers given them by

[7] From an article by Gordon C. Zahn, a graduate student at the Catholic University of America. *Catholic World.* 173:346-51. August 1951. Reprinted by permission.

the electorate to translate the official party platform into legislative reality to the fullest extent possible.

For when a man runs for office on either the Republican or Democratic ticket, the voter has a full right to assume that the candidate is committed to the platform approved by the majority of the party in convention—unless, as in the case of the Dixiecrats, for example, the candidate makes a public disavowal of particular provisions of that platform.

A man who gains election on a platform he does not intend to support actively has obtained his office under false pretenses. Therefore, since both major parties are committed to civil rights legislation, it follows that the majority of the members of Congress are committed to such legislation. There may be some, of course, who have undergone a true change in convictions. It is safe to assume that such instances are rare and, when they do occur, should be honestly and publicly announced by the individual concerned.

In general, it is not unfair to say that failure to produce civil rights legislation can only mean that (a) members obtained their offices under false pretenses, or (b) members are shirking their responsibility to promote the legislation actively.

There is, of course, no defense for the first group. The others, however, may claim that extenuating circumstances render active promotion of civil rights politically inopportune or imprudent. Unfortunately, political prudence has a tendency to degenerate into the lesser "virtue" of political expediency. Every now and again it should be stressed that fortitude is also a political virtue.

It is difficult to justify the appeals to prudence as an explanation of the absence of civil rights legislation. In

the first place, civil rights adherents supposedly constitute a majority. Secondly, the time is eminently propitious: the temper of public opinion would favor legislative protection of the rights of racial and religious minorities, as is best evidenced by the fact that both major parties did consider it a "good" issue to include in their platforms.

Even the traditionally slow-moving Supreme Court has seen fit to act to limit or prohibit racial injustices practiced in certain areas of the country; in 1950, the Court had a far better record in this regard than did the elected legislature.

Finally, *it is the height of imprudence not to push the cause of civil rights* at a moment in history when the world is locked in an ideological struggle in which the support of the non-white populations of Asia may ultimately determine the victor.

But even if such were not the case, even if advocates of civil rights legislation were in a hopeless minority and the American public were solid in its acceptance of continued racial injustice, prudence would still demand an active fight. Instead of subscribing to a compromise of silence, those who were committed to the necessary reform would be under the familiar obligation to be instant in rebuke, in season and out of season.

The more hopeless the outlook, the more urgent would be the need for someone to play the role of "the importunate man" and continue knocking at the door until it was finally opened. The legislator has a twofold function: the construction of a just framework of law and the furnishing of inspiration and leadership to a sound and enlightened public opinion on current issues. When he finds it impossible to accomplish the first task, it be-

comes all the more incumbent upon him to concentrate on the second.

This fact has been sadly neglected in the matter of civil rights. Even those Democrats and Republicans who have not engaged in the actual frustration of attempts to gain passage of adequate legislation joined in a compromise of silence—the first group desiring "to keep peace in the party" and the other seeking to embarrass the dominant party with an eye fixed on the 1952 elections. Neither of these questionable political gains can justify the continuation of injustice!

The report is in on the Eighty-first Congress and, I submit, it convicts that Congress of a lack of political integrity on this most vital issue. The question now rises: will the Eighty-second Congress do any better? Unfortunately, the impression seems justified that a spirit of complete resignation prevails. Even those men we might expect to lead a civil rights crusade, even a hopeless crusade, seem willing to surrender without a fight.

At the moment it seems reasonable to forecast that the final verdict on the Eighty-second Congress will be more unfavorable than the one just passed on its predecessor. At least the latter made a respectable show of trying to get some legislation on the books.

The issue resolves itself ultimately into a question of leadership. Civil rights must be lifted above partisan politics, and this can only be done through the formation of a working coalition of pro-civil rights Republicans and Democrats.

Since the moral question of political integrity is involved, might it not be possible for some Catholic representatives and senators—from both political parties—to join with Protestant and Jewish members of both parties and undertake joint and active sponsorship of an adequate program? These could take up where Marcantonio left off, and they would have the advantage of being above suspicion of "subversive" intentions. (One might even suggest that the Catholic member who now occupies what was Mr. Marcantonio's seat in Congress has something of a special obligation in this regard.) . . .

It has been stated that racial injustice is a great source of strength for the Communist movement here and abroad; yet one is dismayed to find that the Senate FEPC bill, a joint offering of a dozen Republican Senators, conspicuously lacks the name of the . . . Senator who has assumed the role of America's chief scourge of communism!

It is a grave mistake to think, as many do seem to think, that the civil rights issue interests only those minorities that are adversely affected by existing injustices. Its appeal is far more extensive. All who are opposed to bigotry and all forms of injustice born of bigotry are interested in the civil rights issue. Nor is this the total scope of interest. Anyone who believes in political integrity on the part of political parties and their members will be interested in civil rights as a standard by which integrity can be measured. It cannot be repeated too often that both major parties are clearly on record in favor of civil rights legislation—*in everything but action.*

This is a matter that should concern the public just as deeply as do corruption, graft and defamatory campaign tactics. Unfortunately, the evil in recent sensational disclosures is more clearly recognized and the guilt more easily assigned than is the case involving "sins of omission," such as the civil rights betrayal, which are less dramatic and involve a collective guilt.

Nor would it be fair to suggest that all are equally to blame. Rather, the individual share of the collective guilt varies greatly from the legislator who willfully disregards or contravenes his party's platform to his less culpable colleague who honestly laments the failure of Congress to keep faith with the voters but neglects to act decisively to remedy the fault.

One conclusion is clear, however: no one can claim to have done enough, so long as the halls of Congress remain silent while solemn political commitments continue unfulfilled.

The robes of Lincoln are wearing thin on our present crop of Republicans, and the bright promises of the Truman Democrats are fading fast. If there is more than a touch of bitterness to the plaint that "the civil rights issue was no more than a political football," it is perhaps justified. Those who have placed their faith in political action are taking a second look at their idols; and many are learning that shining armor tarnishes all too easily and the feet seem to be made of clay after all.

THE BIG DANGER IS APATHY TO CORRUPTION [8]

The traveler in America encounters worried men. Their primary concern is with the life-or-death issue of war or peace. Their secondary concern is whether we have become morally bankrupt; a race of frauds, givers and takers of bribes, cutters of corners, breakers of laws, gangster ridden, on a huge scale. Some, contemplating the dimensions of the problem, become apathetic. Others, grown cynical, say, "I might as well get mine." Still others wonder how they can rear children to be decent citizens in an atmosphere of corruption. . . .

[8] From an article by David L. Cohn, author of books and articles on the American scene. New York *Times Magazine*. p 10+. October 28, 1951. Reprinted by permission.

Rightly or wrongly, many businessmen believe they cannot do business in Washington without the aid of a "man of influence," one who only yesterday perhaps was a government official. Here, too, the RFC investigation conducted by the Fulbright committee gives color of fact to the belief.

Elsewhere the citizen notes that Federal offices are sold for a price; as in Mississippi where two persons have been convicted of this offense and ten more await trial. He observes that Congress is investigating the Bureau of Internal Revenue upon suspicion that some of its officials protect makers of fraudulent income tax returns. This infuriates him since he, an honest man, is held to strict account for his income tax, while the load evaded by the favored crook is shifted to his back. . . .

But are we morally better or worse than we were in the good old days to which we fondly turn when disillusioned? No one can precisely answer this question. There are no comparable data of measurement as there are of crop production. Who keeps the statistics of bribery, "influence," sharp practices? Yet if it should appear that we are perhaps morally better today than we were yesterday, we cannot derive solace from the fact. A little corruption in government is too much corruption. . . .

Is the Federal Government more or less corrupt than it was in the good old days? Since we have fought two world wars within a generation, let us compare our times with the days of the Civil War. In 1863 the Springfield *Republican*, editorially summarizing House reports, said:

A bureau of the Treasury Department made a house of seduction and prostitution. Members of Congress putting their mistresses into clerkships. An honorable Senator knocked down in the street by a woman he had outraged. Whisky drinking ad libitum. The Government cheated in contracts and openly robbed by its employees. Writes our most careful correspondent, a long resident at the capital, "Washington was never quite so villainously corrupt as at the present time. In the balmy days of Southern rule, of slavery, there was not half the corruption there is now."

The New York *Herald* complained that men were making millions selling bad beef, bad coffee, and broken-down horses to the government. And Carl Sandburg in his *Abraham Lincoln* says that

> . . . a special investigator for [Secretary of War] Stanton inspected many bureaus, examined thousands of witnesses and reported his deliberate conviction that at least 20 per cent, if not 25 per cent, of government expenditures during the war were tainted with fraud.

Union contractors, not satisfied with initial high profits, increased them by delivering shoddy goods to the Army. General James Grant Wilson wrote:

> In tents, a lighter cloth or a few inches off the size; in saddles, inferior material and workmanship; in shoes, paper soles, straw and weeds; . . . and so on through the entire list. . . . Every contractor had to be watched and quartermasters and inspectors stood in for a share of the profit.

In President Grant's days the government sank perhaps to an all-time low of corruption. There was widespread evidence of bribery of congressmen. There were railroad scandals, financial scandals, tariff scandals, land-grant scandals; an atmosphere of legislative degradation prevailed. The Spanish-American War was marked by its "embalmed beef" scandal; while at that time, as before, the country was subjected to the unrestricted selling of fake stocks, fake patent medicines, adulterated food and drugs.

By contrast with much of the past seventy-five years, this period, whatever its skullduggeries, seems almost blithely innocent. Ours has, moreover, been a time of world wars and as *Blackwood's Magazine*, an English publication, said during our Civil War, "A great war always creates more scoundrels than it kills." War is not only wasteful but it is also, for many men, a moral holiday, its almost inevitable concomitant being a breakdown of morals in numerous fields.

Since 1917 we have spent upward of $400 billion for war. One must believe that some part of this incomprehensible sum was stolen by men in and out of government; and also by soldiers in the field. Some men, among millions of men, are bound to succumb to temptation in the face of billions quickly spent without possibility of minute supervision. Yet it is to the honor of the nation that the spending of these billions has resulted in no major scandal.

Staggering sums continue to be spent by the Truman Administration but without major scandal—a fact pointed up by the featuring in the national press of the famous mink coat found by the Senate investigation of the RFC. This is not to say that Washington is entirely incorruptible. It is to say that, considering the hugeness of the government, its complexity, the billions of dollars with which it deals, the discovered corruption, at least, is tiny.

It must be remembered that the government has a large number of agencies policing it, including the Congress; it works in the glare of publicity; members of the minority party, for political reasons if no other, are constantly vigilant to detect wrongdoing within it, while the majority party, as in the RFC investigation and the continuing inquiries of the Armed Services Committee, is no less vigilant in this respect. Paradoxically, then, the very size of the Federal Government and its complexity, far from making corruption easy, make it difficult.

Proof of this is to be found in the widespread corruption, as dramatically revealed by the Kefauver committee, which prevails in many of our state, county and city governments. These are local and localized governments. They are much smaller than the Federal establishment, less complex, and their expenditures, smaller too, are less urgent than those of Washington. Citizens are closer to these agencies than they are to Washington and are aware of their workings to an extent impossible to citizens contemplating Washington. One might think, for these reasons, that local governments could be kept relatively "pure." Yet this, as we know through so many investigations and scandals, is often not true.

Many of the conditions depicted nearly fifty years ago by Lincoln Steffens in his *The Shame of the Cities* prevail today in some of our greatest cities, the principal difference being that the place of the crude, old-time plunderer has been taken by the skillful, highly organized gangster of these times. Here again is local government, and it is here, rather than at the national level, that we are most derelict morally. Yet even here we have not descended so far as we did in the Tweed Ring days of New York, nor are state governments the pawn of railroads as many of them once were.

In numerous fields we have made great progress since the Civil War. The consumer once shopped under the rule of "Let the buyer beware," and unscrupulous merchants used the most ingenious means to cheat him. But the rule of "Let the seller beware" has long been in vogue and has been extended so far as to comprise the principle that "The customer is always right." The overwhelming majority of manufacturers and merchants nowadays make and sell honest products; the customer may generally get back his money if he is not satisfied with his purchase; the one-price system, relatively new among us, rules out a battle of wits between buyer and seller, with the seller at an advantage.

Adulteration of food and drink is forbidden by Federal and state laws. Railroads no longer grant secret rebates to favored customers. Liquor interests are not as free as formerly to subsidize saloons and pollute politics. Child labor is forbidden. The private employment of convict labor, a one-time shame of the South, is presently barred. Private management does not terrorize labor as it once did, while the professional strikebreaker, with his company of thugs, is practically a thing of the past.

Certainly, there is still corruption among us, in high places and low. Some of it is of a crude kind, such as the bribing of police officers. Some of it is more subtle, as the use of "influence" in obtaining loans or other favors from the Federal Government, many of the acts being legally impeccable but morally dubious. None the less, a student of American affairs might well conclude that we have made many moral advances over the practices of our forebears and certainly are far from being morally bankrupt.

We must, however, proceed on the ground that even a little corruption is too much corruption, and I would especially urge upon my countrymen the sage counsel of Governor [Joseph Wingate] Folk of Missouri.

Insisting that bribery is no ordinary felony, but treason, he said that "the corruption which breaks out here and there and now and then" tends to change the form of our government from one that is representative of all the people to an oligarchy representative of special interests. This being true, severe penalties ought to be inflicted upon bribers as well as the bribed. Bribers are perhaps the more reprehensible because, if not gangsters, they are so-called respectable corporations or individuals who strongly tempt the modestly paid public servant.

The glory of our political system is its local and localized self-government. It is here—to use a noble, old-fashioned word—weakest in virtue. The Federal Government is, I believe, clean on the whole, and distinguished by the presence of devoted public servants, many of whom could earn larger salaries outside the government than in it. It is indeed not too much to say, considering the maledictions constantly heaped upon them as "bureaucrats" and worse, that we have in them perhaps a more devoted body of public servants than we deserve.

Undoubtedly there is some dishonor among us, and the present Administration is certainly not free of it. The hackles of the honest citizen rise when he notes it, even though he may think nothing of "fixing" a traffic ticket or patronizing the black market. Governmental dishonor is the more shocking to us because we, to a degree unknown elsewhere, regard men as fundamentally good and are horrified when we find this is not always true. . .

Yet we shall get nowhere merely by denouncing "those fellows in Washington." Capital and nation being inseparable, one may ask, for example, whether "entertainment" began in Washington or was imported from outside. How many manufacturers send gifts to department store buyers? How many entertain them lavishly when they come to market? How many hundreds of millions are annually spent by business for "entertainment"—dollars charged against income tax?

If, then, gift-giving and entertaining are common devices used by business, and if these devices are imported by it into Washintgon, shall we say that the one is entirely guiltless and the other entirely guilty? Even if you should conclude that the "influenced" official is the more guilty since he functions under oath, is the businessman not also guilty of at least attempted subornation? How, then, does it befit him to denounce "those fellows in Washington" when he has been a party to their degradation? . . .

Each generation being prone to regard its times as the worst of all times, it is well to keep our heads as we note the political corruption of these days. If there is dishonor among us, there is also honor. Observe, for example, that the permanent civil service of Washington is singularly free of charges of corruption, these being leveled almost entirely against politically appointed—and therefore transient—civil servants. A reading of our history, it seems to me, would indicate that while our public morality is far from impeccable, it is an improvement over the morality of much of our past. Our greatest shortcoming is not political corruption. It is our indifference toward it, our almost narcotic apathy in its presence, that is our dangerous defect.

CAUSES AND REMEDIES

EDITOR'S INTRODUCTION

If political ethics do not represent a high standard of moral conduct, the question of cause or causes and appropriate remedies must be examined. Generally speaking, the *causes* fall into two categories: (1) the inevitable conflict between *public* and *private* interest and, (2) as Herbert Hoover puts it, the absence or loss of the *old* virtues of integrity, truth, and honor in public officials. It should be noted, however, that all writers agree that a high moral standard of conduct on the part of public officials is very desirable, if it can be achieved.

The remedies suggested by the several writers follow the cause advanced by each proponent. For example, Pendleton Herring contends that the cause is the conflict between Public and Private interest. His remedy includes the need for a constructive presidential leadership plus an administrative advisory body. Furthermore, he contends that both ideas, if they are to succeed, must rest on uncorrupted and responsive officials plus an informed citizenry. Stuart Chase recommends a strong presidential administration in order to "handle" the various powerful pressure groups.

August Heckscher, in his article on ethics and public life, agrees with Pendleton Herring and Stuart Chase on the cause, but he advocates a code of ethics for all public servants and insists that the voter must learn to distinguish between what he calls the *myth* (ideal) and reality.

Senators Paul H. Douglas and J. William Fulbright favor a code of ethics, while President Harry S. Truman calls for publication of all sources of income of public officials.

Dorothy Thompson suggests the election of "good" men to office, while the *Christian Century* editorial criticizes codes because such rules recognize moral disintegration and attempt to adapt to it.

Margaret Hickey and Erwin D. Canham present specific ideas on what women can do to improve the political ethics in local and national elections.

Finally, as an example of what can be done, Alistair Cooke describes the code of ethics as it operates in Great Britain.

THE WHY OF PRESSURE GROUPS [1]

Pressure groups have long been "the despair of patriots." They have been responsible for some of the darkest days in Washington. Some of them engineered the Hawley-Smoot tariff bill, which raised so high a wall that few imports could scale it, at a time when we were a creditor nation. Others put over the Silver Purchase Act, which made it virtually impossible to use our great silver hoard to serve industrial wartime needs. They were responsible for the Chinese Exclusion Act. They killed bill after bill to help the consumer of drugs and foods. They have jammed through bonus grabs, and the totally inadequate tax bill of 1944. They continually pervert, twist and halt the path of progress in the Republic.

Yet some sort of group representation is necessary in a democracy such as ours. Congressmen are elected on a geographical basis. But technology has changed the meaning of geography—and postwar airways are going

[1] From *Democracy under Pressure,* by Stuart Chase, economist and author of books and articles on social problems. Twentieth Century Fund. New York. 1945. p9-20. Reprinted by permission.

to change it a lot more. Today industrial, trade, professional, wage-earning interests are often more important than geographical. But they have no specific representation.

The pressure groups which are the despair of patriots are not a sudden calamity. They grew up with the country, like soil erosion. They are the direct result of certain economic developments and tensions.

A hundred years ago in the "atomistic society" which Adam Smith described, business units were small and fluid. I think of them as a kind of overgrown blacksmith's shop, or the village general store. My home town of Redding, Connecticut, in 1830 had seven fulling mills to bleach homespun cloth on the little streams. Today the town's one factory employs several times as many workers as all seven together.

Prices were largely determined on a free market by supply and demand. No concern was large enough to dominate the market in most things, or even influence it very much. A wide dispersal of self-sufficient family farms provided a safety net. When times were hard, a man could go back to the farm. There was always food there if one was willing to work. The age of scarcity was no Utopia, but chronic unemployment was unknown, and the ups and downs of the business cycle were not the giant roller coaster of recent years.

The first half of the nineteenth century was the heyday of the competitive system. Such trade monopolies as had existed earlier were broken up. . . . Labor unions were treated as conspiracies, and ruthlessly suppressed. A few public utilities were classed as legitimate monopolies and run by the government, but private interests often operated the town water supply, the gasworks, even the roads and schools.

With the development of the railroads in the 1840's and 1850's, a huge new industry was added to the economic system, one which was in many respects a natural monopoly. Railroads widened markets to a continental scale. Bigger markets called for bigger firms and bigger blocks of capital. The fluid atomistic society began to thicken into monopolistic lumps. The "trusts" were forming in the United States, and combinations and cartels in Europe.

The rise of technology, which had brought the locomotive, was also responsible for the large-scale refining operations which led by logical stages to the Standard Oil Company. It was responsible for other new monopolies. But sometimes trusts were deliberately formed to protect the large new capital structures against the ravages of price cutting. The United States Steel Corporation was organized as a kind of legal umbrella under which the companies in the combine were made reasonably immune from competitors. . . .

Wise old Adam Smith, even while he celebrated free competition, was aware that human nature seems to be frequently allergic to its charms. "People of the same trade," he said, "seldom meet together, even for merriment and diversion, but the conversation ends in a conspiracy against the public, and in some contrivance to raise prices." He might have been referring to the famous "Gary dinners," to be held in America a century and more later, which did so much to soften the rigors of competition in the steel business.

Industrial lobbies have been operating ever since the Republic was founded. The Constitution itself was in part a compromise among interest groups. Manufacturers began pressing for tariff protection while Washington was still president. Protection and free land were the two great government handouts of the nineteenth century. The hearts of congressmen were torn with the plight of "infant industries," threatened with unfair competition from the "pauper labor" of Europe and Asia. The tariffs were granted. They were in effect subsidies which made big business bigger, and strengthened its monopolistic position. Once a tariff was granted, a lobby had to be maintained at Washington to see that it was never lowered—to say nothing of seeing what might be done about raising it higher.

A monopoly as such exerts economic pressure on the community, restricting output or holding up prices. When in addition it employs a lobby to look after its political interests, it becomes a full-fledged pressure group. In lobbying for tariffs, various monopolies often joined to form a super-group, the favorite vehicle being the National Association of Manufacturers. . . .

By the turn of the century, these large aggregations of capital had workers pretty well at their mercy. The time clock was on the wall; no longer did the master know all his men by their first names. Furthermore, it was harder to find a farm to bail into when times were hard. One-crop agriculture was undermining the self-sufficient farm. Free land in the West was about gone.

The industrial worker was on the spot. If he was not to become a helot, he had to organize a pressure group to offset the pressure of the "trusts." He did, in the person of Samuel Gompers. The AFL, under Gompers' dynamic direction, shed all ideological goals and concentrated on blasting out of the hands of management exclusive control of wages, hours and working conditions. The AFL grew up with the trusts of the 1890's, though several laps behind them. The railroad brotherhoods were growing too.

In due course, when their votes could really talk, labor leaders descended on the government for their own particular line of tariffs, subsidies and benefits. They wanted the legal right to organize, to picket, to strike. They wanted minimum wage laws, maximum hours, railroad retirement pensions, workmen's compensaton, full crew laws, child labor restrictions, embargoes on immigrants, the exemption of unions from taxation.

Gradually the governments, state and federal, gave the unions much of what they wanted. In the Wagner Act of 1935 they got something very impressive indeed. They could now stand up and slug it out with big business. They could make even such unreconstructed anti-unionists as Henry Ford and Tom Girdler bend the knee.

Observe what has happened to the atomistic society. Bargaining for wages is no longer in the hands of the free individual. It has become "collective bargaining," wherever the unions are active. The term is revealing: the free wage market has ceased to exist. Sometimes the monopolistic trend was carried a step further with the enforcement of the closed shop. So the business blocs came to represent one wing of production, the owner-managers, while the labor blocs represented another wing. The interest of all of us, as consumers, had no bloc to represent it.

The farmers were still inadequately organized when . . . [World War I] came. That war boosted agricultural income, as . . . [World War II] is doing. Hogs, wheat and land values went over the moon. In 1920, the whole structure collapsed. In 1921, the Farm Bureau Federation organized the farm bloc in Congress. Thus the third major producer interest of the country became a specific pressure group.

The farmers moved on Washington, suspicious of "Wall Street" on the one hand, and "labor agitators" on the other. Beyond their own economic strength, they had two great sources of power.

In the first place, they symbolized the ancient, homely virtues—thrift, hard work, the soil, the old well sweep, the rugged independence of the great open spaces. These virtues made excellent camouflage for the hard-boiled commercial drive behind the bloc. In the second place, the geographical election of congressmen gave agricultural states a big mathematical advantage, especially in the Senate. Though dirt farmers accounted for perhaps a fifth of the population, they could, when organized, swing nearly half the votes in Congress.

In the 1920's, the embattled agriculturists got a thin line of relatively cheap government credit, some assorted tariff protection, and many fine information services from the Department of Agriculture. In the 1930's, like labor, they really went to town. They got the AAA [Agricultural Adjustment Administration] for big farmers, the FSA [Farm Security Administration] for little farmers, legislation for an ever-normal granary, crop insurance, farm mortgage relief, cheaper credit, the Food Stamp Plan, and many other benefits. . . . The farm bloc has engineered the major crops like cotton and corn into a position where prices are pegged and output restricted under the shelter of the Federal Government.

Thus large chunks of agriculture, which enjoyed—or endured, if you prefer—a maximum of free competition as late as 1932, have been hoisted clear out of the free market to become in effect state-sponsored monopolies. Historians are going to stand amazed at the rapidity of this revolutionary change in American agriculture.

Big Business, Big Labor and Big Agriculture have all organized monopolies after their fashion and left the fluid play of free competitive forces far behind them. In support of their organized economic interests, each has established powerful political lobbies to bring pressure on both Federal and state governments. Political action followed economic action. The organization of labor followed the organization of business. The organization of agriculture followed both. The whole process has moved with the inevitability of a Greek drama.

There are no lobbies representing the whole consumer interest. The National Consumers League has been concerned chiefly with labor legislation. The Townsend Plan represents old folks, without too much regard for the rest of us. The American Legion represents veterans, with even less regard. Special groups of consumers have lobbies in Washington, some weak, some strong; but no pressure group so far as I know is looking out for all of us. . . .

Besides the special interests which want something, usually with a dollar sign in front of it, for their crowd, there are the reformers. They put pressure on Congress too. . . . The Civil Liberties Union, . . . the League of Women Voters, . . . [and similar organizations are pressure groups which may] have their ideological pitfalls, yet they are the hallmark of a dynamic democracy. They represent people who are not satisfied with the status quo, who want to make it a better country and are not interested in the pay-off for themselves.

Most special interest groups have a formula which tends to freeze the economy. Not only do they want the government to interfere on their behalf, but they want a *high unit price rather than high production.* This leads straight to restriction of output, to scarcity economics, cramps and spasms.

The farm bloc fights for "parity"—the relationship of prices obtaining before . . . [World War I]. The labor unions fight for high hourly rates rather than a rate of annual earnings which would keep them producing steadily throughout the year. Business interests normally have their eyes on all the traffic will bear, holding production to that level.

This is not only against the public interest, in that it keeps the national output below full employment and capacity operation, but it can be very bad business. It neglects the so-called "Ingersoll Dollar Watch formula." Ingersoll reversed the scarcity motive. He figured he could make more by selling a lot of watches at a low price, than by selling a few at a high price. Ford built up his Model T business on the same basis. It made him for a time the richest man on earth. The TVA used the formula when it set very low rates for electric power. The large volume resulting from the policy automatically decreased unit costs to the point where the low rates were profitable. As the Dollar Watch formula puts the accent always on increased production, it leads directly to high levels of employment.

Businessmen as a rule have been afraid of the high-volume–low-price idea. Perhaps it requires too much imagination. It certainly requires faith in one's product, and willingness to take a certain amount of risk. Big business would often rather play safe. Security with a regular conventional dividend is the goal. So it usually instructs its agents to campaign for relatively high prices and relatively restrained output. The whole cartel system is chained to that policy. The Ingersoll idea gets a big hand at annual banquets, but on weekdays management often takes the opposite course. So do organized labor, the farm bloc, the mining interests, and the rest.

With the Big Three—business, labor, agriculture—all organized in an impressive way, the typical congressman has his troubles. In a clash, whom will he support? Here is the Hon. Clarence Cannon of Missouri, apparently requested by William Green of the AFL to vote for the subsidy bill. Mr. Cannon searches his heart and comes up with this classic reaction: "I have always followed Mr. Green on labor bills. But this is not a labor bill. This is a farm bill. On this bill I follow the farm leaders." . . .

The rise of the Big Three as outlined above warrants two conclusions. *First,* the pressure groups between them have pretty well demolished the free market as Adam Smith pictured it. *Second,* it is clear that a state dedicated to laissez faire can remain a passive umpire only so long as organizations are small. When Big Business, Big Unions and Big Farmers moved in upon the government, the community had to develop the Big State to cope with them. E. H. Carr summarizes it this way:

> Every modern state has intervened, first, to protect employers against trade unions, and, later to protect the rights of the unions. If we wish to get a correct picture of the structure of the modern world, we must think not of a number of individuals . . . but of a number of large and powerful groups, sometimes competing, sometimes cooperating, in the pursuit of their group interests, and of a state constantly impelled to increase the strength and scope of its authority in order to maintain the necessary minimum of cohesion in the social fabric. . . . The issue is whether to allow social action to depend on the haphazard outcome of a struggle between interest groups or to control and coordinate the activities of these groups in the interest of the community.

This is putting the present crisis of political democracy about as flatly as it can be put. It comes down to the question of who's in charge around here? If the pressure group free-for-all holds the stage, economic breakdown is not far away. If the government is in charge, there is the danger of the authoritarian state. Yet if a breakdown develops, the danger of the authoritarian state immediately reappears, and in a more extreme form.

We are not expounding theories. Even Germany was a democracy once. . . .

With Congressman Doaks looking for the high sign as to how he shall vote from Ed O'Neal, from the AFL man, from the NAM lobbyist—and getting pretty cross-eyed in the process—we have about stopped counting on him to represent the whole community. Who does look out for all of us?

There are two answers: we ourselves, and the president of the United States. Neither is a very good answer—not nearly so good as it should be. As individual citizens most of us are adolescent Americans. Our country has been so vast, so rich in natural resources, that it has never occurred to us until lately that anybody needed to be responsible for keeping it going. It is clear, however, that the more responsibility we accept as individuals, the less needs to be taken by the government. If, for instance, all the 40 million Americans who drive cars should suddenly begin taking heed for the anatomy of their neighbors, think of the decline in traffic cops, judges, courts, public ambulances and hospitals!

As Walter Lippmann has pointed out, the only agency which officially represents all of us is the presidency—the president himself and his executive aides, including at present a number of special bureaus. As a matter of fact, the president seems to have been cast in this role by the Founding Fathers. Congressmen were supposed to represent the states and localities. Only the president could look over the heads of the clashing local interests and see the nation, steadily and whole. That, at least, was the theory, and there is something in it. If flesh-and-blood presidents did not have to devote so much time to trying to get reelected, there might be even more.

In these days, when pressure groups have turned Congress into a sort of revolving door, the necessity for the executive to represent all of us becomes even more urgent. Is this generally recognized and allowed for? It is not. On the contrary, the executive arm is labeled "bureaucracy," and lives in a perpetual blizzard of criticism. This makes it difficult to get the mail signed, let alone do any intensive representing of the whole community.

Intensive representing we must have, however, if the pressure groups are to be controlled. We must have a watchdog devoted to the interest of all the people. As long as the people do not get together and instruct their hired agents, they depend on volunteers, or on chance. In a way, the president acts as a volunteer when he analyzes a public demand and takes action to satisfy it. Sometimes a congressional committee, like Senator Truman's, acts voluntarily in the public interest, not in response to a definite mandate, but with wide approval once it has acted. Such an administrative bureau as the late National Resources Planning Board was created to assist the president (and presumably Congress as well) in studying the consumer interest. Such a bureau as the Farm Security Administration was created to represent a class of farmers who were not articulate enough to apply much pressure, but who badly needed help.

If it were a question of deciding among petitioners, the president would have little difficulty in balancing the pressure groups. Now, however, it has gone beyond that stage. It has become a matter of curbing power which already is overgrown. Nobody, to my knowledge, has the specific task of curbing that power, or even of planning how to curb it.

If the government were so organized as to give legitimate representation to economic interests, the pressure groups could never have grown so strong. But our government is not so organized, as we have repeatedly noted. Today industrial, trade, professional, occupational interests are often more important than the geographical interests which are supposed to limit congressmen.

This is one reason why many congressmen consider it their duty to represent economic interests which are strong in their states–so that we talk of "Silver" senators and "Cotton" Ed Smith. The lobbies of these interests take care that the duty shall not be too painful to the congressmen. Such representing has to be done, however, with a good deal of indirection, because technically Congress is not supposed to take any action favoring special interests.

The relations of government to business, labor, and farmer are intricate beyond description. . . . There is constant give and take. Does government run business in the War Production Board or do businessmen run government? Both statements are true in part. Does government run the farms or does the farm bloc run government? In giving labor more power, has government weakened its own position? And by government do we mean Congress, the president, the war control boards, or the great departments? We have to look beneath the high abstraction, "Government," in order to find meaning in this powerhouse of clanking gears.

PUBLIC ADMINISTRATION AND THE PUBLIC INTEREST [2]

Administration in a Democracy

Under democracy the public interest is based not upon the welfare of one class but upon a compounding of many group interests. We assume the possibility of achieving a balance of forces, social and economic. Whether this process becomes anything more than political jugglery depends upon the standards of justice that are accorded general acceptance by the community. Will social responsibility and loyalty to the democratic process outweigh opportunism and immediate self-interest? Intrinsically this is a question for statesmen, but officials can affect in some measure the turning of the scales.

The administrative branch of the government cannot maintain a balance in a dynamic society but it can do much toward clarifying and effectuating the purposes declared by our legislators. The caliber of our officials and the efficiency of their organization will largely determine the successful application of those policies designed to promote the general welfare. An able administrative service has much to offer. If the state is to carry its increasing burdens, the potentialities of officialdom must be realized to the utmost. . . .

Economic laissez faire is gone; political laissez faire is passing. The government is undertaking the care of groups that are economically insecure; it is defending interests that are politically weak. Can a democratic

[2] From *Public Administration and the Public Interest*, by Pendleton Herring, President of the Social Science Research Council and formerly Associate Professor of Government, Harvard University. McGraw Hill Book Co. New York. 1936. p vii-viii, 7-9, 18-27, 347-8, 385-9, 394-9. Reprinted by permission.

government interpret in such positive and specific terms the meaning of the general welfare regardless of the strength of the underlying interest groups? In theory our government should strike a balance among these conflicting forces so as to promote the welfare of all. In fact some groups are placed more advantageously than others within our governmental structure and under our industrial system. The government draws its strength from the very elements it is supposed to regulate. Its officials both elective and appointive are subjected to constant pressures from these powerful interests. Complete objectivity is practically impossible for the elective official. It exposes the administrative official to the charge of bureaucratic aloofness. Our government must be responsive if democracy is to survive. Yet the citizen in facing public questions seeks to promote his own immediate interests rather than the welfare of all. This attitude becomes the more dangerous as government extends its activities further into the social and industrial life of the nation.

What the final outcome of such tendencies will be no one can say. The authoritarianism of fascism and the dictatorship of the proletariat are the two alternatives persistently offered. Before granting the inevitability of either, the possibilities of our present democratic institutions warrant further exploration. . . .

Administrative experience . . . gives cause for hope as well as fear. Weaknesses, abuses, and failures are frequently found. But experimentation continues. No logical a priori theory can embrace the flux of actual government. New laws, new administrative forms appear. There is a persistent search for some workable means of adjusting the forms of governance to the uneasy needs of men. The story of the Federal bureaucracy today is kept in a looseleaf ledger. Revision is the only constant. In this lies the hope for the future. . . .

Bureaucracy and Democratic Government

Congress has to an increasing extent escaped the onus of directly settling group conflicts by establishing under vague legislative mandates independent regulatory boards. The technical and complex nature of these conflicts has encouraged this trend. A parallel development within the past two decades has been the great increase in the service activities of the Federal Government. Bureaus have been established to aid special classes and sections and have thereby given all interests strong enough to demand it a share in public funds and services. Moreover, under emergency conditions, and where the political pressure has been very great, direct aid and subsidies have been distributed. Thus has the democratic process redressed the balance among conflicting interests and avoided arousing to the point of rebellion groups adversely affected by the ruthless force of a competitive society.

Upon the shoulders of the bureaucrat has been placed in large part the burden of reconciling group differences and making effective and workable the economic and social compromises arrived at through the legislative process. Thus Congress passes a statute setting forth a general principle. The details must be filled in by supplemental regulation. The bureaucrat is left to decide as to the conditions that necessitate the law's application. He is in a better position than the legislators to perform these duties. His daily occupation brings him into direct contact with the situation the law is intended to meet. He knows what can be enforced and he can better envisage the limits of legislative fiats. This increase in administrative discretion, while making possible the more understanding application of rules to concrete situations, nevertheless places a heavy duty on the administrator. The words of the statute delimit his scope, but within the margin of his discretion he must write his interpretation of state purpose.

The social and economic aspects of this process must be left to others. The political result has been the preservation thus far of the liberal democratic state as the agency of control and the transfer from Congress of much of the direct superintendence of reconciling the conflicting groups within the state. The governmental result has been the creation of a great bureaucracy with wide powers to carry on these functions. Great public services are needed all the way from the primary functions relating to police, sanitation, and the care of paupers to official enterprises that compete with private business. . . . The extent to which these activities are carried cannot be fixed but will vary in accordance with the character of the economic groups that have succeeded in attaining control of the government at any given time. There persists, nevertheless, a residue of responsibility no matter what combination is in control of the government. The mere existence of a great administrative organization necessitates a certain continuity that has little reference to political overturns. Groups must be willing to recognize that the state has a purpose which transcends their own immediate ends. The bureaucracy cannot assert a state purpose against the united hostility of groups that basically comprise the source whence authority springs.

In the United States the bureaucracy suffers for want of a hierarchical organization and a personnel united by a harmonious concept of state service. But a bureaucracy in these terms arouses the suspicion and criticism of interest groups, who regard the administration as designed to serve them or at least *not to interfere* with their group purposes. And it is these interest groups that wield political authority under a representative system. Such interests criticize "bureaucracy" as inimical to popular government. Yet only through developing a proper administrative organization can democracy survive.

We conclude, then, that the purpose of the democratic state is the free reconciliation of group interests and that the attainment of this end necessitates the development of a great administrative machine. Thus, paradoxical as it may seem to Jeffersonian Democrats, the liberal democratic state must be sustained by a huge bureaucracy. This viewpoint, however, has not won general acceptance. . . .

Bringing Democracy into Administration

Does democracy under modern conditions mean nothing more than the doubtful duty of choosing at intervals between the ballyhoo of the "outs" and the balderdash of the "ins"? . . .

If politics is to mean anything to the average man, it must speak in terms that he can understand. He must be able to meet "government" upon his own level and speak to the "governors" in the language of his profession or business. If contact with the governing process is confined to the periodic casting of a ballot, democracy is sterile indeed. Any numskull can put his cross on a slip of paper and drop it in the ballot box. We have need of Aristotle's conception of citizenship wherein direct participation in government was the determining factor.

We have learned the limitations of direct democracy. Our experience with the direct primary, the initiative, the referendum and the recall, and the long ballot have demonstrated that the mass public cannot be treated as though it possessed a unified and responsible will. We have been largely preoccupied with manipulating the elective and legislative aspects of government. The election of representatives and the framing of laws by these spokesmen are but the initial phases in the process of popular control. It is in the execution of the laws that government assumes direct and concrete meaning for the citizen. Popular responsibility must then be broken down to conform with the relevant interest units of the community. The choice lies between this and either control by a political party or bureaucratic isolation.

These latter alternatives are the handmaids of dictatorship. There can be no responsibility of the mass of officials to the mass of the public. The chief executive is perhaps the only figure who can be thought of as holding a general mandate from the people. If the administration of laws is left in the hands of a bureaucracy that is not accountable for its actions, representative institutions become farces. The sporadic and tardy intervention of a legislative body in the affairs of the executive branch is inadequate as a check upon the bureaucracy. This is particularly the case under the presidential system in the United States where the independence of the executive and the remote relations of the cabinet members to Congress render effective surveillance difficult. . . .

The problem is twofold: (1) to keep the bureaucrat responsive and uncorrupted; (2) to join the citizen with the administrative process in order to utilize his particular expertness or to gain the sanction of his consent. Herein lies the meaning of modern democratic government. It is in these terms that public administration must be faced if "popular control" is to have any meaning for this present age. If the democratic process is to continue, it must be guarded, not simply by exhorting the citizen to his duty, but by making guardianship part of the duty of officials. Opinion is like water. Administrators must dig for it. In only a few instances does it rise spontaneously and even then the source may be tainted. A storm of disapproval may bring a downpour of protest upon officialdom, but flashes of indignation are as transitory as they are sudden. A sustained interest is more desirable.

The main rule, according to [Harold J.] Laski, is that "officials should do their work in the atmosphere of a critical and competent public opinion." This is the only reliable safeguard against the dangers to which bureaucracy is prone. Competent and intelligent administrative services have conscientiously conducted the business of the state in other countries, but, when they have become remote from the opinions and concerns of those they governed, grave abuses have inevitably appeared. Even though the public service is directed by honest men endowed with *esprit de corps,* inflexibility and unimaginative routinism threaten when contacts with the public outside cease to be close and sympathetic.

Interest groups are here of great aid in showing congressmen administrative needs and in convincing them of the "public" support behind such requests. These special-interest groups are much better acquainted with administrative problems and with the records of officials than are the legislators. Since the heads of administrative departments and bureaus hold no positions of power in the legislature, they must seek support outside. Owing to the lack of an integrating device, such as the ministry, it is difficult to obtain remedial legislation directly or to bring about a change in policy through statutory declaration without political assistance. By working hand in hand with pressure groups, officials immensely strengthen their position before Congress. "These same group forces must be looked upon," one authority states, "as furnishing a political check upon a powerful Executive with discretion to put into effect or to suspend laws in particular cases, to turn the purpose of Congress in directions not contemplated by that body, or to create privileges and rights as well as to take them away."

Inescapably the bureaucrat becomes the target of pressure groups. He is, to be sure, in a more defensible position than the congressman whose public career may be cut short by the powerful enmity of organized interests. Nevertheless, these groups, because of conditions peculiar to our present administrative system, are of great personal significance to public officials in this country. The future of many civil servants, particularly the ablest and most enterprising, lies not in the Federal service but in the private employ of the groups with which their official duties bring them into contact.

Security of tenure for the administrator has been cited as a needed safeguard against political interference and group pressures. The official must undoubtedly be able to resist intervention when it is aimed at procuring privileged treatment. The bureaucrat, however, does not suffer so much from an inability to execute the law unhampered as from an uncertainty in direction. Where is the official to look for guidance on the broad plain of public interest? He is hemmed in by the immediacy of his own tasks. Within the system of which he is but a subordinate part, his contribution to the total administrative responsibility is left largely to his own judgment. . . .

What criteria are to guide him? The *public interest* is the standard that guides the administrator in executing the law. This is the verbal symbol designed to introduce unity, order, and objectivity into administration.

This concept is to the bureaucracy what the "due process" clause is to the judiciary. Its abstract meaning is vague but its application has far-reaching effects. The radio commissioners were to execute the law in the "public interest, convenience or necessity." The trade commissioners are to apply the law when they deem such action "to the interest of the public." Congress has frequently authorized boards and quasi-judicial commissions to determine the public interest.

Although it is clear that the official must balance the interests of the conflicting groups before him, by what standards is he to weigh their demands? To hold out the *public interest* as a criterion is to offer an imponderable. Its value is psychological and does not extend beyond the significance that each responsible civil servant must find in the phrase for himself. Acting in accordance with this subjective conception and bounded by his statutory competence, the bureaucrat selects from the special interests before him a combination to which he gives official sanction. Thus inescapably in practice the concept of public interest is given substance by its identification with the interests of certain groups. . . .

The predicament of the bureaucrat now becomes clear. Special interests cannot be denied a voice in the councils of state since it is their concerns that provide the substance out of which the public welfare is formulated. On the other hand, a well-coordinated and responsible bureaucracy is essential if the purpose of the state is to be attained. The solution of the liberal democratic state must lie in establishing a working relationship between the bureaucrats and special interests—a relationship that will enable the former to carry out the purpose of the state and the latter to realize their own ends. . . .

Public administration in actual practice is a process whereby one individual acting in an official capacity and in accordance with his interpretation of his legal responsibility applies a statute to another individual who is in a legally subordinate position. The public as such is not concerned in this process.

To the officer executing the law, the public is simply an abstraction. Law is applied by one man to another. In the realm of discussion, the public is treated as a reality and words are directed to the populace. But this is a one-sided relationship. Officials receive many responses from individuals but the only reaction they receive from the public is that which they may choose to read into a collection of individual reactions.

Generally these responses may be arranged in more precise categories built around an occupational or economic interest. When this happens, the official finds it possible to negotiate with groups articulate and self-conscious because of a common concern.

Thus law is not administered in a vacuum, but in an environment composed of all those who have an interest in the application or the nonenforcement of the statute. The official is surrounded by a web of interests—and a web often dominated by an unpredictable spider. This ultimate determinator may be the courts, the legislature, an administrative superior, or a powerful economic interest. The administrator is one strand in a complicated mesh of forces, political, social, and economic. . . .

What Can Be Done?

The question raised is this: What can be done toward the clarification of the public interest within the bounds set by our political framework? . . . The possibility of reorganizing the Federal administration depends upon an understanding of the social forces and group pressures that stand in the way.

As a practical matter, what the theorist might regard as ideally best in administrative organization must be reconciled with what is politically possible. Democracy means that our Federal structure shall be the product of what politically effective individuals and groups are able to get. If the government is to act as an impartial arbiter among all groups and if the administration is to serve all classes and interests, how can this be accomplished in the face of our political structure?

Congress has displayed little understanding of such problems, but an enlightened bureaucracy and constructive presidential leadership can do much toward improving administrative conditions. . . . Coordination in the Federal administration is not altogether dependent upon the pressure of interested groups. Officials can seek to clarify the interests of those classes that are represented by important bureaus and departments. Through coordinating devices they can mobilize those elements that are of intrinsic social import but meager political strength. These agencies will enable officials to look beyond their limited jurisdictions and participate in the pursuit of common objectives. This is one way toward administration in the public interest. . . .

The fact that a spontaneous and coherent public opinion cannot arise to solve political problems does not mean that popular government is impossible. It means rather that our governmental institutions must be fitted to the limited capacity of the citizen to participate in political decisions. If the public can do no more than indicate assent or dissent, the clear presentation of alternatives becomes of the utmost importance. The offering of positive proposals by a responsible administration is then the first goal to seek. Especially during the Roosevelt administration has the office of the chief executive acted as a clearing office for new theories and proposals. Suggestions have come from hard-headed and often socially nearsighted men of affairs and from imaginative and often impractical men of theory. The President has picked up items here and there and, working with an informal group of advisers, official and unofficial, has drawn up legislation for congressional action.

The increased power of the president means, of course, an increase in the importance of the bureaucracy. Consistency in the formulation of presidential policy involves an intelligent and efficient arangement of the whole administration service. This is recognized by the greatly increased demand during the last decade for administrative reorganization and civil service reform. . . . Another objective of modern democracy, then, is the development of a competent bureauracy.

If the existence of the democratic regime rests upon the assumption that the state exists not for the welfare of any one class but for the benefit of the people as a whole, this great and growing bureaucracy must be guarded from domination by economic groups or social classes. On the other hand, it must be kept free of the abuses of aloof, arbitrary, and irresponsible behavior to which public servants are so often prone. . . .

One of the most striking characteristics of our government is the chasm that exists between the administrative and the legislative branches. Here is separation not merely of powers but also of sympathies and viewpoints. Those who man the two branches do not speak the same language. They think in different terms. Congressmen look upon the bureaucracy with more suspicion and distrust than understanding and respect. It is the rare legislator who knows much about the actual operations of our departments and bureaus or who appreciates their problems.

The congressmen who have served for years upon certain committees in the course of time learn about the administrative agencies that come within the province of these committees. But theirs is a partial view and it is not shared by the changing rank and file of the House and Senate. To maintain his seat a legislator must know his constituency and the needs of his section; he has little time left for a study of the Federal administrative offices. Moreover, the congressman strives to meet the demands for legislative action made by his constituents. As a representative, this is his job. Suggestions, however, coming from such interested parties have little connection with the broad needs of the country and little understanding of the administrative task of carrying the proopsal into effect. We cannot afford to enact a mass of sporadic and uncoordinated legislation.

Laws are now more and more frequently formulated in the administrative offices. They are sponsored by congressmen and senators who have more faith than understanding. This shift makes a responsible bureaucracy all the more urgent. It also makes it highly desirable that the representative factor be introduced into the administrative process. The compromise of group interests and the formulation of the actual terms of the legislation should be worked out largely in negotiation between administrators and the interested parties and then submitted to the legislature for criticism and discussion. . . .

Administrators are in a more secure position than the elected representatives, however. They can cope with lobbyists on a relatively secure footing. Moreover, their special knowledge enables them to understand the merits of proposed legislation in terms of what is possible of enforcement and of accomplishment. Neither special interests nor the bureaucracy are able to decide the major question of policy—should this bill be passed? This must remain a legislative problem. But the form of the enactment and the pros and cons of the issue can best be understood by those directly in touch with the problem under consideration.

If the expert knowledge of special-interest representatives and that of the bureaucrat are combined, some workable solution can generally be found. Agreement at this point forestalls opposition later in Congress. Private parties in consultation with experts in the government must agree upon a course of action. The detailed and technical provisions of a bill can thus be discussed by those most competent to deal with these questions. The difficulty at present is that measures drawn up by administrators in consultation with outside experts and interested parties are opened up for amendment in Congress by legislators seeking to curry political favor. Such activities would be discouraged by placing more directly the responsibility for formulating legislation in the administration and by seeking to disarm the conflict of sections and of classes by compromise in advisory committees.

Of course, differences will remain, and the right of opposition will mean that democratic government continues. Our goal is not the eradication of all disagreement but rather the expression of a stated purpose by a responsible agency expert in character and in close touch with the realities of the situation that must be met. If Congress wishes to go its own way, it remains free to do so, but it is thereby put on the defensive and its decisions are open to the suspicious scrutiny of the administration, the public, and the special interests allied with the presidential program. . . .

How can a program be formulated for the promotion of the general welfare and carried into effect consistently and justly? There is no final answer to this problem. Sweeping constitutional changes may be necessary. The partial answer offered . . . [here] points to the contribution that might be drawn from the administrative branch. The lines that may be followed are summarized in these four words: clarification, consultation, cooperation, and coordination.

Clarification stresses the administrative duty of collecting pertinent facts, relating them to the task to be met, and then presenting these findings to the public. It is, for example, the duty of the State Department to study foreign affairs and to explain its decisions clearly. The Coordinator of Transportation studied his problem thoroughly and then presented his conclusions so that all might read. The graphic reports of the recent Committee on Economic Security showed a commendable effort to place the need for old-age pensions and unemployment insurance before the public. Research and publicity for this research must go hand in hand.

Consultation with the persons and groups most directly concerned must likewise become a regular feature of administration. This is the greatest safeguard against arbitrary or ill-considered action. The practice of hearings and conferences is fairly general. Such contacts should be made more systematic. Official recognition of lay interests should be carried further. The Business Advisory and Planning Council is a hesitant step in the right direction.

As consultative agencies are developed, a greater degree of cooperation between government and private organizations is made possible. The National Advisory Committee on Aeronautics shows how experts inside and outside the administration can join forces. Officials, by deliberately developing close contacts with the groups under their general jurisdiction, can maintain public confidence and act for the best interests of the parties concerned.

To realize the public interest in public administration, however, it is necessary to coordinate the activities of officials. Under any system of administrative organization there will always be activities that cut across the established lines. A thorough reorganization of the Federal Government would reduce but by no means eliminate these interdepartmental lines. The need persists, then, of finding some point for coordinating these activities that escape integration within their respective departments. Under our present illogical arrangement this need is especially pressing. As already noted, a few Federal departments serve to coordinate the interests of those classes politically strong enough to secure such departments. For other interests special agencies such as the Central Statistical Board of the Science Advisory Board suggest another means. . . .

An Advance toward Administration

An administrative advisory body with a membership embracing all the interests falling within the jurisdiction of the Federal Government might be developed gradually. It would serve as a means of harmonizing administrative action within the statutory terms set by Congress. It could discover contradictory purposes. It could evaluate the relative importance of various bureaus. It could pass upon the projects offered by the research and planning agencies in the various departments or commissions. It could include officials and laymen in its membership. The latter would be selected by the consultative agencies allied to the government to give expert advice on questions relating to health, education, transportation, labor, industry, etc. The former would speak as experts for their respective departments or commissions.

The council would be occupied chiefly in considering internal administrative problems and in integrating the work of the various bureaus. It might be used as a recruiting ground for the formation of interdepartmental committees to study special problems. Special subcommittees might be formed to investigate and report confidentially to the president. Building up an administrative council in the future would mean little more than encouraging a process that is already under way. The parts of the whole are scattered here and there in various departments. Where advisory committees do not actually exist, still the practice of informal consultation is generally established. As the powers and duties of administrators develop, they must arrange in more substantial fashion their relations with special interests. To this end administrative advisory committees should be extended more systematically throughout the Federal services.

These committees would be composed of representatives from the special interests with which a particular bureau is concerned. These committeemen would be technically competent to advise, but not legally authorized to commit their industry or profession to the support of any governmental policy. Such spokesmen might be selected from a panel made up by the appropriate organizations of interests having regular contacts with a particular bureau. These committees would form part of an administrative advisory council. Its chief usefulness would be in coordinating the work of various branches within the administrative services and in cooperating with private interests.

The council in plenary session would serve as an open forum for the exchange of viewpoints and the discussion of problems submitted to it by the president. Administrators could thus learn what their fellows are doing and planning. *Ad hoc* committees might be appointed from this body to consider special problems and offer confidential advice to the bureaus immediately affected. Above all, the council should avoid any appearance of duplicating the duties of Congress. Its first responsibility would be to discover how the laws passed by Congress could be most effectively and harmoniously executed.

Some device for "grasping this sorry scheme of things entire" is certainly needed. Our experiments with emergency councils, advisory councils, and consultative committees all point to the possibility of developing these agencies further. A general administrative council, closely joined to the White House secretariat and aided by consultative committees in special fields, could be readily realized.

Some sort of administrative council or general staff for the Federal Government has won wide acceptance in theory and in principle. Opinions differ as to its precise composition and duties. Specific suggestions as to organization and function are given in the final report of the National Planning Board. This study recommends a body of five members to be appointed by the president for an indeterminate tenure. They would be assisted by experts selected from a rotating panel. This panel would include "men or women from various groups able to contribute to national planning—as governmental bureaus, labor, agriculture, industry, the home, technical and scientific societies, and other groups directly concerned with the sound formulation of the lines of our national progress." This would initiate inquiries on emerging national problems; it would seek to coordinate various planning activities of other Federal agencies and provide information on all planning projects. The report makes this very important point:

> It cannnot be too strongly emphasized that the function of such a board as proposed is not that of making final decisions upon broad questions of national policy—a responsibility which rests firmly upon the elected representatives of the people of the United States. Such a board would be useful in proportion as it was detached from immediate political power and responsibility, as a general staff gathering and analyzing facts, observing the interrelation and administration of broad policies, proposing from time to time alternate lines of national procedure, based upon thorough inquiry and mature consideration, constantly preparing and presenting to the authorities its impressions, findings, conclusions, and recommendations for such disposition as those entrusted with governmental responsibility may deem appropriate.

A planning council, if it is to be a body for deciding policy, must either supersede the president and Congress as formulators of policy or become a fifth wheel on the governmental machine. We discard as chimerical and impractical a super-planning board that will tell the country what to do. . . .

The government of the democratic state reflects inescapably the underlying interest groups of society, but the very fact that the state exists evinces a basic community of purpose. National rivalries or the operation of economic forces imperfectly comprehended may result in conditions that threaten the livelihood of certain classes. In guarding their own self-interest these classes may be willing to sacrifice that form of government whose keystone is toleration. Those seeking self-preservation are little concerned with guarding the democratic ideal. If a strong class interest can be identified with the continuance of democracy, so much the better.

The bureaucracy of the future should have as its most immediate interest the preservation of the democratic regime. The higher the intelligence, the training, and the devotion of this corps, the greater will be the likelihood of its fulfilling the essential duty of making the democratic state function. Of course, the danger remains that possibly the bureaucracy may ally itself with capital or with labor and so bring about the rule of fascism or communism. But this is by no means an inherent defect. There is no reason for thinking that governmental servants are bound together by an inner necessity that predisposes them to any one economic or social interest. . . .

The government must undertake the coordination of its numerous activities and the planning of further developments in such clear and unequivocal terms that the citizen can perform his elementary duty of voting yea or nay. In the executive branch lies the task of confronting the people generally with an interpretation of the public interest that they can accept or reject through the established channels of representative government. It is thus that a positive view of politics can be attained by the man in the street.

The essence of democracy lies in the freedom it allows all citizens to voice an opinion concerning how and by whom they shall be governed. It recognizes the right of all to consider the welfare of all. What is in the public interest is thus a common problem.

For some years to come the voter will have to consider what aspects of the general welfare the Federal Government should properly take under its jurisdiction. The administrative aspects of this shift cannot be ignored. Whether the Federal Government should assume more or less responsibility for the general welfare is a highly debatable point. But what cannot be gainsaid is the necessity of accommodating the administrative machinery to its burden. At the present time this machinery is inadequate in many ways. Many of its imperfections are due to weaknesses inherent in democracy itself. . . .

More bureaucracy does not necessarily mean the death of democracy, but it does involve some essential readjustment. In recent years changes have been acclerated by economic stringency. It has been difficult to see clearly the direction of many trends. Old phrases have been used to discredit developments that deserve more careful analysis. No solution lies in damning bureaucracy while at the same time increasing the administrative duties of the Federal Government. The litter in Washington must be examined piece by piece. Are we ready to pay the price for federal participation and control?

The New Deal has not invented this question, but recent events have sharpened the issue. It is an issue designed to raise the devil politically; but such demons cannot be exorcised by the mumbo-jumbo of slogans. Forms of government must accord with social needs. Constitutionalism is not an end in itself. In this country it is a method of government upheld by a grave weight of tradition and the merits of great accomplishment. The ultimate justification of the United States Constitution lies in this—that its specific provisions harmonize with the high purpose expressed in its preamble.

ETHICS IN PUBLIC LIFE [3]

It can be set down as generalization, only slightly exaggerated, that Americans spend more time talking about corruption in government, and do less about it, than any other people on earth. In the past year and a half three congressional investigations have filled the newspapers for weeks on end with lurid and picturesque details. Senator Hoey's inquiry into the operations of the "five per-centers," Senator Fulbright's investigation of the Reconstruction Finance Corporation, and Senator Kefauver's investigation of the widespread links between politics and organized crime, have loomed as major events upon the domestic scene. The use of television in bringing the Kefauver hearings into millions of homes has added a fresh intensity and a new dimension to public indignation. Yet if past experience is a guide, the sound and fury will signify, at best, only a minor and temporary change in the standards of public conduct.

To say that Americans enjoy the sight of corruption would be to overstate the case, though there is no denying that figures like Frank Costello and Virginia Hill, flushed from the underbrush of the nation's life, can act out a striking and instructive scene. They have the simple appeal of characters in a morality play. Both the puritan and the rebel against puritanism, the acknowledged sinner and the pharisee, can observe them with satisfaction. . . .

To a greater extent than it is enjoyable, however, corruption in government has become an accepted factor in the operation of our two-party system. It is the lever by which the opposition musters the enthusiasm and the

[3] From article by August Heckscher, editorial writer for the New York *Herald Tribune*. *Yale Review*. 40:577-91. June 1951. Reprinted by permission.

popular support to replace the men in power. Even on the national level differences of principle and ideology between the great parties are so ill-defined, and discipline is so loose, that a case is difficult to argue on rational grounds. "Turn the rascals out!" is the most effective of all campaign cries. If Truman's popularity sank in March of the year to its lowest ebb, the tale of a mink coat and of a government official's few weeks spent free in an expensive Florida hotel probably had more to do with it than fumbling in the domestic or international fields.

On the municipal level the charge of corruption is, of course, even more effective as a political weapon, because venality is likely to exist there in a greater degree; and more necessary, because the opposing parties are so lacking in coherent programs. . . .

This stress on corruption as a political weapon is not new. Walter Lippmann, writing his first book in 1913, pointed out the deadening effect it could exert. "Politics," he asserted in his opening sentence, "does not exist for the sake of demonstrating the superior righteousness of anybody." He described as "one of the great American superstitions" the idea that politics is a contest between good men and bad. Yet in large measure it has continued through the years to be regarded as precisely this, with the result that politicians have been spared the effort of focusing their minds upon creative proposals or fertile issues. At the same time, as recent disclosures make amply plain, the extent of corruption has not noticeably diminished.

It will not diminish, I am convinced, so long as we continue for various reasons to deal with it solely on the political level. Campaigns may be waged and won on the issue of corruption, but the general situation is virtually unchanged. Each party may be vigilant in picking out flaws in its opponent, but it overlooks the flaws in its own ranks; and the rascals, being turned out, are superseded by new rascals of an identical breed. That the public acquiesces in this game of musical chairs is indicated by its traditional cynicism about politicians. Recent polls have shown that roughly seventy per cent of the people believe it impossible for a professional politician to be honest, and that only twenty per cent would want their sons to enter on political careers. With this attitude, the public can hardly suppose that it is striking any very effective blow for morality when it grows fiercely indignant, hotly self-righteous, and then substitutes one group of politicians for another.

In real life, of course, partisanship is almost always stronger than a sense of moral outrage. It is striking that the two most recent investigations have been conducted by members of the same party as the administration in power—Senator Fulbright's and Senator Kefauver's. But this is an exceptional state of affairs; and even in these cases there was an observable reluctance to push the investigations to their conclusion once it was apparent how much they were damaging the Democratic cause.

The usual pattern of exposure is for the opposition to conduct fishing expeditions on the slightest pretext. The result, as Woodrow Wilson pointed out, is that the Congress does not deal with the administration except to disgrace it. Another result is that the party tends to rally around a member under attack, no matter how grave the charges against him. . . .

The conflict between dealing with corruption by popular action and dealing with it by intrinsic checks is indicated by the record of Congress in disciplining its own members. The obligation of the separate Houses to maintain standards of decorum and rectitude is imposed by the Constitution; it should be reinforced by the jealousy with which the two bodies guard their prestige. Yet the record in this respect is lamentable. In an important study, Professor H. H. Wilson has recently traced out a number of contemporary instances. In the House one member was censured (but not expelled); four failed even to have cognizance taken of their alleged unethical conduct. The Senate shows up only slightly better. . . .

The responsiblity has been evaded in part because of the atmosphere of good fellowship, the disposition to uphold one another at all costs, which pervades any American association or club and is frequently strong in parliamentary bodies. More fundamental, however, is the argument that the removal of members charged with unethical conduct is an action for their own constituents to take. It is in other words, a political issue. . . .

If the issue of corruption is to be dealt with in a practical way, and not merely talked about or used as a political football, much study and hard thinking will be required. Understanding will have to take the place of emotionalism. Corruption in government is sometimes, of course, a result of weakness and plain dishonesty on the part of individuals; but it is also the result of conditions and circumstances which make the run of men more vulnerable at one time than another. To know the points at which dishonesty most frequently shows itself, to understand the forces that permit even ordinarily reputable men to become ensnared, is to work the beginning of the cure. When we know where to be especially vigilant, we can prevent the occasional misdeed from building itself up into a web of evil; and when we have analyzed the institutional framework of graft, we can create standards which all but the deliberately unethical will observe. Where departures from the standard take place, the public will then have a sound basis for appraisal and judgment.

The beginning of any analysis of what might be called the anatomy of graft is the realization that it most frequently occurs in those areas of public life where the myth and the reality fail to coincide. For example: under Prohibition, the myth was that the country had forsworn the use of intoxicating beverages; the reality was that people went on drinking very much as before. The bridge between fiction and fact was created by the bootlegger and by all those who were drawn into his conspiracy. The outlawing of betting, while betting still continues as a major industry, is but one more example of what might be a long catalogue to account for the graft that riddles virtually every metropolitan police force. . . .

The most general and notorious form of corruption in the first part of the century arose from the efforts of big business to dominate state legislatures and, to an only slightly less degree, the national Congress. Investigation after investigation revealed the work of lobbies in securing the passage of laws favorable to business interests, and even in securing strategic committee appointments. How this form of corruption arose, why it was so insidious and prevalent, becomes clear when we recall to what extent business called the tune for all aspects of American life in that day. What was good for business was, without question, good for the country; it was good also for the arts, for education, for philosophy and religion. Was it not, therefore, in Lincoln Steffens' phrase, "natural, inevitable and possibly right" that by corruption or some other means business should "get and be the government"?

Unfortunately there were few who viewed the situation with Steffens' lucid disenchantment. The people still saw the government as being exclusively concerned with business. They refused to recognize the existence of that shadowy common ground where both necessarily had interests—where the business lobbies held out their bribes and the people's representatives did their undercover work.

Today the relationship between business and government is infinitely more complex. The administrative agencies have introduced a wholly new factor; the supremacy of the interest of business has been severely challenged; and the legislator plays a new role in the total picture. If all this could be seen clearly, without being clouded by memories or false assumptions, the problem of graft in its modern forms could be understood and ultimately dealt with. As an example of a field where fresh thinking needs to be done, I cite the relationships between congressmen and the heads of administrative agencies. How are contracts between them to be governed? What limits and principles are to guide them in dealing with one another?

The old assumption is that the two branches of the government are separate. Congress frames the laws, and, except for checks to see that they are being properly executed, leaves the administrators a free hand. In practice, however, the congressman is tempted to interfere more or less regularly. He is urged by his constituents to see why a certain contract for war production has not been awarded; to expedite the granting of a license by the Federal Communications Commission; to push a loan or to secure a visa. No congressman would think he was fulfilling his duty if he turned a deaf ear to such requests, and the more ebullient among them pride themselves on going far beyond that. . . .

The answer to this situation is not to reaffirm the separation of powers and then close our eyes to the practical means by which such separation is nullified. It is, rather, to explore the relationships which are necessary to the smooth working of government, to define them, to regularize them, and to set standards from which only the plainly dishonest will be inclined to depart.

It would seem to begin with the realization that a congressman has a right to intervene with an administrative agency where he feels some injustice has been done or some major inefficiency perpetrated. It would seem justifiable to transmit a request from a constituent—though the mere suggestion that a number of congressmen wrote letters to the RFC on behalf of loans to their constituents has raised an odor of scandal. Beyond this, there are evidently limits to which the congressman cannot go with propriety.

Senator Paul Douglas, who has given much thought to the problem, sums up his own code of action in this way:

> The legislator should be courteous and gentlemanly in his dealings with administrative officials. He should never threaten them with reprisals if they turn him down, nor offer promises of help if they favor him. The issues should be presented to officials on their merits, and it should be made clear that the administrator is to have the final decision in the individual case.

Senator Douglas adds that neither a legislator nor any member of his family should receive any favors or jobs from people or corporations for whom he has intervened. These may seem like general rules, but they suggest an approach to one source of corruption which may be immeasurably more fertile of results than spasmodic fits of public indignation released after the harm has been done.

A similar analysis can be made of the role of the administrator. The neutrality of the administrative force has been assumed by traditional political thinkers. Separated from the legislature, aloof from the economic groups whose affairs he regulates, the bureaucrat has been supposed to exist in a kind of vacuum, applying impartially the rule which the legislator lays down. In fact, however, he has had to interpret the rule; he has very often had to improvise it; and the guides to his conduct have had to come from contact with economic life. The concept of a detached bureaucracy, drawn as in France and Britain mainly from one class of the population and with its officials frequently drawn for several generations from the same family, has for various reasons never been at home in the United States. The civil service itself was a late development. The functions of government were restricted far beyond their counterparts in Europe. And when a bureaucracy was first established, it was not, as in Britain, shaped to the needs of empire. For all its shortcomings, and for all the arrogance which individual bureaucrats may show, the administrative branch in the United States has had the task—not of ruling—but of organizing and regulating. It has, as a matter of course, been tied in closely with business leadership and business groups.

The moral postulates of the past have called for a monk-like abstention from the market place. Practical necessities and expectations have required first-hand knowledge and a fundamental sympathy with the aims of the group being regulated. Is it any wonder that a whole area of contacts and relationships has grown up largely unanalyzed and unlighted by appropriate ethical considerations? . . .

The awarding of war contracts has proved especially difficult from the moral point of view. Administrative officers in this field have not merely had to resist enormous pressures; they have also had to stir up trade. A major general who figured prominently in the news during the Mead investigation defended his presence at an elaborate wedding given by the Garssons on the grounds that "it was desirable to keep up the morale and maintain the vigor of all those war contractors." Obviously that was a little steep; but it can be maintained that something more than disinterested aloofness was required of the effective administrator in that period.

The code governing such relationships would probably turn out to be a matter of common sense. The administrator would be expected to do his business in office hours, not at bars, or at cocktail parties, or on the golf course. He would be expected to refuse all gifts from those with whom he had official dealing—whether at Christmas or any other time. He should not accept an offer of employment in a private business whose case had come before him, at least for a specified period after leaving government employ. Such rules could be extended on the basis of evidence turned up in recent hearings. What is significant is that until now rules of this kind have not been promulgated at all; it has been assumed that simple moral postulates, or the injunctions of the criminal code, could cover all the intricacies of a changing human relationship.

One further area in which the reality and the myth have parted company, thus opening the way to a moral void, may be mentioned briefly. It is the position of the businessman vis-a-vis government. The businessman and the government administrator have been thought of as eternal opposites, two races of men with a great gulf between. In recent years, however, there has been an increasing tendency for businessmen to go in and out of government, as consultants, as dollar-a-year men, as administrators undertaking a specific task. The edges of the two worlds have also been blurred by the hiring by business of government administrators. Instead of the hostility which theory presupposes we find the affairs of government being ordered and regulated to a significant degree by business leaders, while business is carried on by ex-officials of the government. Nice questions of ethics inevitably arise; they have been left for the consciences of individual men to resolve.

That an official should divest himself of financial connections and interests which might affect or be affected by his work is obvious; yet it is not always easy to define the limits of this rule. Mr. Edwin W. Pauley defended his dealings on the grain market while he was serving as Mr. Truman's special ambassador on the grounds that no special knowledge, not available to the public, had been made use of. Senator Elmer Thomas, then ranking Democratic member of the Senate Agricultural Committee and General Wallace H. Graham, White House physician, defended similar transactions on the grounds that in the one case a wife, and in the other a broker, took the initiative without benefit of any special information that might have come through government channels. The fact that such defenses can seem plausible illustrates the need for more precise standards.

The problem of severing connections with one's private affairs becomes particularly vexing when government officials are drawn more and more from industry, rather than from law, as in former times. In his memoirs Mr. Henry L. Stimson remarks that "during my various excursions into public life I have always felt that I remained a lawyer with a law firm waiting as a home behind me, to which I could return on the completion of my public task and where I would always find awaiting me congenial friends and collaborators." But the practice of law is varied and flexible, permitting the sensitive individual to avoid cases where there might be an overlapping with public duties; and Mr. Stimson was but one of a long line of public servants who have found inner freedom and independence by keeping roots in that profession. It is different, however, when a man is on leave from a high post in a particular corporation. Not only a particular set of values, but contacts and involvements that may become compromising, are carried over in passing between private and public employ.

The hiring of government workers by private industry is a normal procedure (though it is doubtful whether in any previous generation industry would have found the bureaucracy a source of talent); yet it can lead to abuses if not brought within the moral code. A business seeking some advantage from the government has in the offer of lucrative employment a powerful means for influence in an official. The official, on the other hand, can bring with him to the business the benefits of an "inside track" to his former agency. At the minimum it ought to be established that businessmen must avoid employing men with whom they have had dealings in government.

All this provides only suggestions of the kind of research, investigation, and study which must be applied to the whole field of government, if something more than recurrent indignation is to be brought to bear in solving the complicated problem of governmental corruption. The study, as I have tried to indicate, must be tough-minded and realistic, piercing through the inherited assumptions to a recognition of the way modern government actually works. It must arrive at rules which fit existing conditions, and of which the rationale is plain to all except those who are most obtuse morally.

Happily there are signs that we are beginning to move along such lines. The investigation of the "five per-centers"—the flourishing group in Washington which has used "influence" and "pull" to impress the bewildered businessman in search of war contracts—has already resulted in a number of procedural changes which strike at the heart of the problem. Decentralization of contract-making brings the government to the country, rather than bringing the whole business community thronging to the capital. A system of regional offices, combined with a series of local conferences for businessmen, enables the producer to arrange an order without leaving his home district. In addition, many new government contracts include penalties for unwarranted contingent fees. The Senate subcommittee on ethics headed by Senator Douglas will proceed upon lines equally encouraging, and the reports that have been published by the Kefauver committee contain practical proposals for Federal legislation and, equally important, the establishment of ethical standards and principles appealing to the sense of the community.

The sanctions for moral reforms cannot come, in the last analysis, from criminal penalties; except in the case of the most gross and obvious forms of dishonesty, a more flexible approach is needed. Changing methods, and changing ethical concepts within the public mind, must be permitted to play a part in modifying and tempering what is or is not permissible. Only the cynic will suppose that nonlegal sanctions are useless. There are strong forces which work upon the members of any group or profession inducing them to follow the norm, once the norm is accepted and known. Senator Fulbright has viewed with dismay the modern tendency to admit to no compulsions or restraints outside the bounds of strict legality, but if this is so, it is perhaps because there are so many areas where, except for the bare prescriptions of strict legality, there are no meaningful and acknowledged patterns to which the man of average honesty is expected to conform.

In maintaining public morality there is need for a certain shrewdness, a canny appreciation of human nature with all its weaknesses and temptations. To be honest in a particular field of activity must not be made too difficult. Moreover, matters must be so ordered that the comparatively small amount of dishonesty always to be expected will not be fatal, and will not spread by habit or contagion. The founders of our political system were full of clever provisions for counteracting the effects of man's depravity. Vice, as they used to say, must be set against vice; interest must be balanced against interest, so that selfishness itself will become a factor for stability and an ingredient of the general good. Yet it never occurred to former generations that selfishness alone could unite a commonwealth or that without virtue a great nation could be composed. They knew that in the end there must be a preponderance of honest men. There must be a vast majority which at least try to follow rules they believe to be just.

In spite of all the moral degradation, the cheapness, the desire for easy wealth and power that wars and social upheavals have left in their wake, this preponderance of virtue remains. Without that it would be vain to talk about morality in public life—or, for that matter morality in the arts, in education, in the professions, or in the private existences of men and women.

WE NEED A NEW CODE FOR WASHINGTON[4]

Over the centuries we have worked out standards of propriety which judges are supposed to follow in deciding cases that are brought before them. The parties to a case are not supposed to discuss it with the judge outside of the courtroom, and he should resolutely refuse to accept any favor from an actual or potential litigant. The final decision is based solely on evidence produced in the courtroom or submitted in written briefs. Neither legislators, the press nor private citizens should try to influence the judgment before it is given.

While these standards are sometimes more honored in the breach than in the observance, it is well that we should have them. For they do insure a far greater degree of justice than would be the case were judges to jostle and be jostled in the hurly-burly of life. It has, however, been largely possible to achieve this degree of insulation because the volume of court cases is fortunately small in relation to the population, because there is full publicity and argument of opposing counsel in the courtroom and because the decisions of the court must be stated and justified in writing and, except those of the highest court, are subject to appeal.

No such standards have been worked out or applied in the case of administrative officials whose decisions,

[4] From article by United States Senator Paul H. Douglas, Democrat from Illinois. New York *Times Magazine*. p 12+. April 1, 1951. Reprinted by permission.

with the growth of government, now vitally affect, both individually and collectively, the lives of tens of millions. Consider, for a moment, the ways in which the decisions of government officials can make or break the lives of Americans—the men in our armed forces, the millions more who will be on the selective service rolls, the veterans receiving compensation, the thousands in Federal prisons, the people and 400,000 corporations who pay income taxes, the utilities whose rates are fixed by government commissions, the air lines and the broadcasting companies whose range of activity is controlled, the families that receive Federal-state assistance payments, the individuals who receive old-age insurance and farm benefits.

All this is only a partial listing of the persons affected by controls which the government exercises. And in the semi-war economy which Russian aggression has forced us to establish, complex new controls have been set up.

I believe that it has been necessary for government to assume most of the functions it exercises, in order to carry out the general purposes outlined in the preamble to the Constitution; namely, to "establish justice, insure domestic tranquillity, provide for the common defense [and] promote the general welfare." But it is obvious that almost frightening power has been placed in the hands of the officials who make the key decisions both by promulgating the general rules of administrative law and by passing upon the individual cases of application and enforcement.

If these men perform their duties with intelligence, energy, complete integrity, a devotion to the common good, mixed with a sympathetic understanding for the plight of individuals caught in the web of government rules and regulations, the country is greatly benefited.

But if the administration falls into the hands of corrupt, lazy, ignorant or haughty men, the instrumentalities of government can become weapons of oppression and destroyers of human liberty.

Now I believe that on the whole the present level of administration in the national government is fairly high. The main run of government officials show a good deal of public spirit, are reasonably intelligent and energetic and have fairly high standards of integrity. They compare favorably with officials in private business. A few are selfless saints; some, I regret to say, are probably corrupt. Taking human nature as it is, most officials are likely to be somewhat influenced by their prejudices and friends, and some become greedy and corrupt. Initiative and imagination on the part of officials are seldom rewarded and often punished. . . .

When the people decide that the government should take on some new function and Congress sets up an agency to administer it, enthusiasm runs high. The government is then able to get devoted supporters of the principle to take on its direction. These men, backed up by public opinion, will work hard and incorruptibly. For a time all will go well.

But soon ossification and degeneration set in. The early enthusiasts die off or leave government service. Some remain, but lose most of their fire and zeal. The public thinks the battle has been won and turns its attention to other things. The special interests which stand to gain from rulings begin to move in. They designate Washington representatives and set up lobbies. They seek to entertain and to seduce the vital officials. Those who go along with them are rewarded in one form or another. Officials whom they like are, for example, frequently offered jobs at very high salaries in the industry with which they are dealing. This has happened an undue number of times, for example, with the staff and in some cases the members of the Securities and Exchange Commission and the Reconstruction Finance Corporation. It has happened all too often in the case of procurement officers in the armed forces.

While complaisant officials are being rewarded, the obstinate defenders of the public are frequently ignored or punished. Objections are raised by powerful groups to their renomination or promotion. If renominated, efforts are made to "get something on them" so that they may be refused confirmation by the Senate and disgraced.

Once this process of administrative degeneration sets in, it progresses rapidly and in a short space of time an agency which was originally alert and public spirited becomes waterlogged, indolent and corrupt. If we are to preserve the virtues of free government, we must prevent this degenerative disease of officialdom from proceeding further and instead raise the moral standards of government. I believe the revelations by three senatorial investigations of the last two years, namely, that by Senator Hoey into the activities of the "five percenters," by Senator Kefauver and his associates into "organized crime," and by Senator Fulbright's subcommittee on the RFC, have developed both the facts and the necessary public opinion to do this. . . .

I have come to the conclusion that the whole level of government administration would be immeasurably and permanently raised if we were to adopt basic standards of propriety which are to be followed.

These standards could properly be embodied in the Administrative Procedures Act and should deal with the proprieties to be observed by administrative officials, applicants or litigants and their attorneys and representatives, and members of Congress.

It is true that by putting these standards in the Administrative Procedures Act, no criminal sanctions would be imposed upon men who might violate them. The law to that extent would lack "teeth." But the promulgation of this "code" would not only furnish standards as to how the members of these groups should act when they deal with such matters, but it would also give to the press and to the public a clear basis for determining official right from wrong. Moreover, since these standards are primarily intended to deal with the questions of propriety and impropriety, it is perhaps well to begin in this more tentative fashion before fastening such a code on to the harsh structure of the criminal law.

Let us begin, therefore, with a suggested and tentative set of standards for each of the three classes which I have mentioned.

First, so far as government officials and agencies are concerned, I would suggest that all discussion about a private application or claim with an official or unofficial representative of the applicant or claimant, should take place only during working hours and in public buildings. When a case is pending before a quasi-judicial body such as the Interstate Commerce Commission, the Federal Trade Commission, the Securities and Exchange Commission, etc., members of the board which will have to make the ruling should not be approached privately in their chambers by either attorneys for the government or the litigant to discuss the merits of the case, and any such conversations should deal only with procedural matters.

The purpose behind this provision is, of course, to prevent either public or private parties from getting to the ear of a man who sits in a judicial capacity and to insure that there will be no prejudicing of the final decision. Written or oral arguments of one side should only be advanced in the presence of the other with full opportunity for rebuttal by the opposite side.

Second, it should be required that the government agency maintain a docket open to public inspection which would show not only the cases listed but the attorneys and representatives involved. To this should be added all fees paid by the applicants or claimants and any "kickbacks," "finders' fees," or other splitting of fees by these attorneys or representatives. Furthermore, government officials obviously should not accept either favors or gifts of any magnitude from private citizens.

Third, and extremely important, no one in a government agency who deals with the claim of a private concern should accept employment with it for a period of approximately two years. If an attorney once resigns to go into private practice he should not accept a case involving formal appearance before the same agency for a similar period of time. For men are often consciously or unconsciously seduced by the promise or prospect of lucrative private employment when they quit government service. Coming events cast their shadows before.

The one possible exception I would make to this rule is in the case of the Patent Office, scientific in nature and where, if all opportunity to practice before the Patent Office were barred to men leaving its employ, there would be virtually few places outside of government where they could practice their profession.

Private parties dealing with the government should observe reciprocal proprieties. They should not seek to "pressure" government officials outside of working hours, entertain them, or to offer gifts or favors, directly or indirectly, to those in government employ. Similarly, they should list all their representatives before government bodies and furnish full data on the amounts which they receive and disburse. Finally, in appearing before a regulatory, loan-granting agency, they should agree not to offer employment for a stated period of time, say two years, to anyone in the agency who deals with their claim, application or contract.

What, then, should be the standards which legislators should observe in dealing with public officials? There are some public administrators who would seal off legislators from all contact with them and prevent congressmen and senators from taking up any administrative matter. Legislation, they say, is different from administration and should not be mixed with it. In their judgment, paraphrasing Gilbert and Sullivan, "the fingers of learned statesmen should not itch to interfere in matters which they do not understand."

I am convinced that it would be a great mistake to adopt such an extreme position as this. A bureaucracy is almost never critical of its own mistakes and shortcomings. Like most human beings and organizations it tends stubbornly to stick by earlier decisions, even when wrong, and to cover up its errors. The men and women who are underneath the harrows of the bureaucracy and who are pricked by its prongs can seldom get relief through individual complaints. It is small wonder, therefore, that they turn to their congressman or senator for help.

In my Washington and Chicago offices I probably receive close to fifty such appeals a day. Some are unreasonable; some come from people trying to get undue favors; but many are well-grounded and valid. To prevent a legislator from taking up these latter cases would tend to deny justice to countless individuals and would perpetuate administrative abuses and mistakes.

For not only are individuals protected by such congressional inquiries and specific wrongs righted, but from an accumulation of such cases, legislators from time to time become convinced that certain laws or administrative rulings should be changed. The legislative reforms which are then made help whole classes who, save for the prior investigation of individual cases, would never have found relief. On the whole, therefore, I consider the practice of congressional inquiry into individual cases to be one of the best protections which this country has against the dangers of an oppressive, overweaning and callous bureaucracy.

But there are, of course, standards of propriety which the legislators should themselves observe in such matters. Claims which are patently unreasonable should be tactfully discouraged by them. Other inquiries should be investigated by the staff in so far as possible. In this connection, however, the average voter or official does not realize the pressure of work which now pours in upon a Senator or Congressman. For example, I am at present receiving about seven thousand communications and hundreds of telephone calls a week. The senators from New York probably receive many more and conversely, those from smaller states fewer. Everybody, it seems, wants something, and they want immediate attention to be paid to their demands. At best, therefore, only a rough sifting can be given to these complaints and requests.

It is proper, I believe, to refer such complaints to the appropriate government agency for treatment and reply. If the same type of case keeps recurring and the replies of the agency seem unsatisfactory, questions of general policy can then be raised. If, upon a more detailed investigation, a case seems especially meritorious, it is proper to make a courteous recommendation. For since administrative officials properly advise Congress on the revision of laws, it is only fitting that legislators should in turn advise administrators. Interaction between these two agencies of government is far more healthy than complete isolation.

But there are restraints which a legislator should observe. Neither he nor any member of his family should receive any favors or jobs from people or corporations for whom he has intervened. He should be particularly wary to see that friends do not abuse his confidence and try to use him for improper ends. This is frequently the most difficult task of all, for it is commonly a man's friends, rather than his enemies, who get him into trouble. The legislator should be courteous and gentlemanly in his dealings with administrative officials. He should never threaten them with reprisals if they turn him down, nor offer promises of help if they favor him. The issues should be presented to officials on their merits, and it should be made clear that the administrator is to have the final decision in the individual case. . . .

It goes without saying that observance of all the proprieties is not by itself sufficient to guarantee justice, but it can help to eliminate some of the dangers. We must depend also upon the training and selection of government officials to make the public interest paramount, if the basic moral quality of government service is to be raised.

MORAL STANDARDS OF GOVERNMENTAL CONDUCT [5]

When the Subcommittee on the Reconstruction Finance Corporation undertook its study, more than a year ago, I anticipated the development of little more than the usual issues which grow out of an investigation of the executive branch of the government. I expected just another case study of an agency, with a finding of facts to be made and an orthodox legislative remedy recommended.

Before we had proceeded very far, however, it became evident that we were dealing not simply with a legal or legislative problem but with a moral problem. The first case to which my attention was called was one involving the employment, by a borrower, of an RFC employee who had recommended the granting of the loan. The Board of Directors of the RFC thought this practice quite proper. I thought it improper. So from the beginning we were confronted with a difference of ethical standards. It presents a very difficult problem. It is difficult because the evils to be dealt with are so seldom amenable to the processes of law. When confronted with an evil, we Americans are prone to say, "There ought to be a law." But the law does not and cannot apply effectively over wide fields of men's activities. It cannot reach those evils which are subtle and impalpable. Generally speaking it reaches only the overt and the blatant acts of the wicked. . . .

As our study of the RFC progressed, we were confronted more and more with problems of ethical conduct. What should be done about men who do not directly

[5] From a speech by United States Senator J. William Fulbright, Democrat from Arkansas, delivered in the Senate, March 27, 1951. *Vital Speeches of the Day*. 17:386-7. April 15, 1951. Reprinted by permission.

and blatantly sell the favors of their offices for money and so place themselves within the penalties of the law? How do we deal with those who, under the guise of friendship, accept favors which offend the spirit of the law but do not violate its letter?

What of the men outside government who suborn those inside it? They are careful to see that they do not do anything that can be construed as illegal. They operate through lawyers—men who are known as clever lawyers; a cleverness which is like the instinct of the rat that knows how to get bait without getting caught. Many businessmen, ostensibly reputable businessmen, employ these knavish lawyers to circumvent the law and enrich themselves at government expense. Too often the law cannot touch them.

Who is more at fault, the bribed or the bribers? The bribed have been false to their oaths and betrayers of their trust. But they are often relatively simple men—men of small fortune or no fortune at all—and they weaken before the temptations held out to them by the unscrupulous.

Who are the bribers? They are often men who walk the earth lordly and secure; members of good families; respected figures in their communities; graduates of universities. They are, in short, of the privileged minority, and I submit that it is not unreasonable to ask of them that high standard of conduct which their training ought to have engendered. Is it too much to ask of them that they do not use a government lending agency as a dumping ground for their own mistakes in judgment? It it too much to ask of them, the favored few of our country, that they behave with simple honesty; with that honesty which looks, not to the letter of the law, but to its spirit? . . .

The essence of what we have been studying in our committee is but a reflection of what may be seen in many other phases of our national life. The government and its activities are, in a very real sense, a mirror of our national life. The inquiry into the RFC has revealed conditions which unfortunately may be found in other activities of our people.

Let us consider what has developed in our colleges where the characters of our young men and women are being molded. Our colleges, under extreme pressure from the alumni have become so intent upon winning football and basketball games that they use any means to gain their ends. They hire players who are not bona fide students and thus make a mockery, a farce, of the whole concept of amateur sport for the health and entertainment of our young men. They corrupt not only the hired players, but also the entire student body, who learn from their elders the cynical, immoral doctrine that one must win at all costs.

A by-product of this doctrine, this necessity for big money, led naturally to betting and to the shocking episode of the widespread bribery of basketball players in New York. I find it difficult to blame the players. They are but following a logical sequence of influences, beginning with the corruption of the sport at its source by pressure from the alumni.

This question of the moral strength of our people is not just an internal domestic matter. It has grave implications in our international relations. Without confidence in their government, the people will not make the sacrifices necessary to oppose Russia successfully. Professor Toynbee, in his well known historical study, demonstrated clearly how the vast majority of great civilizations have been destroyed, not as a result of external aggression, but as a consequence of domestic corruption. A democracy can recover quickly from physical or economic disaster, but when its moral convictions weaken it becomes easy prey for the demagogue, and the charlatan. Tyranny and oppression then become the order of the day.

I wonder whether in recent years we have unwittingly come to accept the totalitarian concept that the end justifies the means, a concept which is fundamentally and completely antagonistic to a true domestic society. Democracy is, I believe, more likely to be destroyed by the perversion of, or abandonment of, its true moral principles than by armed attack from Russia. The evil and insidious materialism of the Communists is a greater danger to us than their guns.

One of the most disturbing aspects of this problem of moral conduct is the revelation that among so many influential people, morality has become identical with legality. We are certainly in a tragic plight if the accepted standard by which we measure the integrity of a man in public life is that he keep within the letter of the law. . . .

Some weeks ago, I suggested, informally, that it would be beneficial to have a commission of eminent citizens designated by the Congress, to consider the problem of ethical standards of conduct in public affairs. I renew that suggestion now. . . .

Such a commission, as I conceive of it, would be a catalytic agent, stimulated by public indignation, to draw forth meaning from the mass of data revealed by the several current investigations. The commission would evaluate the conditions which have been exposed, and drawing upon its combined wisdom would restate again, or formulate anew, principles which, it is to be hoped, would strengthen the faith of all decent men in our democratic society.

Too many people in our nation do not believe anything with conviction. . . . The values of life which were clear to the Pilgrims and the founding fathers have become dim and fuzzy in outline. False propaganda and the "big lie" of demagogues have created doubt in the minds of men. Professional political hucksters, imported from afar, without local responsibility or restraint, corrupt our free elections and poison democracy at its source. The principal objective of the study I suggest is the restoration of the faith of our people in the validity of the traditional precepts of our democratic society. It is not a job for politicians; it is not a job for the inexperienced; it is a job for the wisest of our citizens under a mandate from the nation. . . .

I confess that I do not know what should be done. If I knew, I would not call upon the wisest men of our country. I would suggest it myself. But . . . I am unwilling to accept the view that nothing can be done, that the moral deterioration, which is so evident to all, must continue, to its logical conclusion, which is the destruction of our free democratic system. . . . I think something can be done.

CONCERNING HONOR IN PUBLIC LIFE [6]

We might explore some of the things that have happened to the old virtues of integrity, truth, and honor in public life. During the recent past we have had a flood

[6] From a speech by Herbert Hoover, former President of the United States, delivered at the Iowa Centennial Celebration, Des Moines, Iowa, August 30, 1951. *Vital Speeches of the Day.* 17:716-18. September 15, 1951. Reprinted by permission.

of exposures by congressional committees, by state legislatures, by grand juries in scores of cities, and the press.

A few days more than 175 years ago, the fifty-six members of the Continental Congress of the United States unanimously declared a program of action and certain principles of American life. The concluding words of the Declaration are a pledge of "our sacred Honor."

I sometimes wonder what the fifty-six fathers, from their invisible presence in our congressional halls, would say about the procession of men in responsible position who have come before its committees of this day. What would they have thought of the "sacred Honor" of the "five per-centers," mink coats, deep freezers and free hotel bills? Or favoritism in government loans and government contracts? Or failures to prosecute evildoers who spread cancerous rackets and gambling rings with their train of bribed officials? . . .

I would like to explore this old virtue of truth, integrity and honor in public life a little further.

Congress can well widen the laws so as to clutch the new kinds of bribes and benefits they have discovered. But Congress cannot reach intellectual dishonors.

Part truth, concealment of public commitments, propaganda and its gadgets and failure to enforce the laws are but part of them. And there are group pressures "to get theirs" which smell from both the decay of integrity and the rotting of patriotism. And some persons arrive at their morals with a divining rod that measures morals in terms of votes.

The Congress, from its own inquiries, is confronted with the fact that sacred Honor cannot always be tested by legality or enforced by law. In its frustration, the

Congress is groping for some sort of code of ethics, which with a prefix "New" might protect the citizen from his own officials.

Might I suggest that there are already some old and tested codes of ethics? There are the Ten Commandments, the Sermon on the Mount, and the rules of the game which we learned at our mother's knee.

Can a nation live if these are not the guides of public life?

Think it over.

The American people have a right to bitter complaint over these disclosures of dishonor in high places. The duty of public men in this Republic is to lead in standards of integrity—both in mind and money.

Dishonor in public life has a double poison. When people are dishonorable in private business, they injure only those with whom they deal or their own chances in the next world. But when there is a lack of honor in government, the morals of the whole people are poisoned.

The drip of such poisons may have nothing to do with dishonor in some college athletics or the occasional policemen on the beat. But the rules of the game have been loosened somewhere.

Some folks seem to think these are necessary evils in a free government. Or that it is smart politics. Those are deadly sleeping pills. No public man can be just a little crooked. There is no such thing as a no-man's-land between honesty and dishonesty. Our strength is not in politics, prices, or production, or price controls. Our strength lies in spiritual concepts. It lies in public sensitiveness to evil.

Much as the Congress has my good wishes, something stronger than a new code of ethics is needed by America. The issue is decency in public life against indecency.

Our greatest danger is not from invasion by foreign armies. Our dangers are that we may commit suicide from within by complaisance with evil. Or by cynical acceptance of dishonor. These evils have defeated nations many times in human history.

The redemption of mankind by America will depend upon our ability to cope with these evils right here at home.

Think about it.

But I do not wish to leave you, the neighbors of my childhood, with any implication of pessimism. I speak to you of some of our weaknesses, not because of frustration or despair, but to urge remedy. The fact that we are vigorously washing our dirty linen in the open is a sign that moral stamina still survives.

Without bitterness in our hearts, we are raising our eyes to the Creator of man who assured us that in American soil we can find the moral and spiritual forces which make free men and women. In His guidance, we shall find the fortitude to correct our errors, to straighten our courses, to resurrect the spirit that made our America so free and bountiful a nation.

For reassurance in the future I need only to turn my thoughts to my grandparents who came to this state in the covered wagon. Here they and my parents toiled that their children might have greater opportunities than had been theirs. Here they worshipped God. Here they lived out their lives in the faith and hope of Americans. They lie buried on an Iowa hillside.

Therefore, here in this state where I was nurtured, I cannot but feel a strength that comes up from the deep roots in the very soil on which we stand. That strength is in character and truth and decent living. And it will triumph.

It will triumph because I know America is turning its face away from the maudlin leftisms and the spread of untruth of the past two decades. We sense the frauds on men's minds and morals. Moral indignation is on the march again.

DEMOCRACY IN THEORY AND PRACTICE [7]

Any thoughtful observer of government in the United States today is forced to report widespread political cynicism and deep distrust of government on all levels, as well as a popular feeling of helplessness, sometimes approaching despair—more often expressing apathy.

During the current year, the Senate Committee to Investigate Organized Crime in the United States (the Kefauver Committee) uncovered appalling situations. It was established that criminal rackets are nationally organized; that in every state gangsters are allied for mutual profit with law-enforcement agencies; that in some places it is difficult to disentangle or even distinguish organized crime from organized government. . . .

Yet the puritan spirit is not dead. A majority of Americans place honesty, integrity and independence of mind above party loyalties and class interests. It has often been demonstrated that voters will break class and party allegiances to support candidates whom they believe to have these qualities. It is not true that "good" men cannot be elected to office. Men who have taken the currently unpopular side of issues have repeatedly been

[7] From article by Dorothy Thompson, noted journalist. *Ladies' Home Journal.* 68:11+. October 1951. Reprinted by special permission from the *Ladies' Home Journal.* Copyright, 1951. The Curtis Publishing Company.

reelected to Congress, simply because the people had respect for their characters.

In every community there are men and women in whose characters, energy and judgment large numbers of people have confidence. They may be newspaper editors, clergymen, businessmen or trade-union leaders. They are on hand for every unofficial movement for community improvement; they do not sway with every wind that blows, but are rooted in character and common sense.

Why is it often difficult to persuade such persons to run for public office?

First, because too few people are trying to persuade them. But such able persons have other doubts. They say, "I am incompetent to play the political leader who dares to run afoul of the 'idols of the market place.' Maybe I could take it, but I don't want my kids coming home from school with black eyes for defending me against what this or that radio commentator may have said about me the day before. You can't exercise good judgment if your chief purpose is to get yourself reelected. And party leaders don't regard character and competence as necessarily the best vote-getting qualities. There are few men in political life today who would dare oppose any measure which has a strongly organized claque behind it."

Since political parties are a fact, the first duty of a citizen, it seems to me, is to join one—and, of the major parties, I don't think it makes a great deal of difference which one. If we leave the composition and control of political parties only to people who have some personal or group interest to promote, we are going to have officials nominated by special interests and under obligation to them. These may be criminal racketeers seeking collusion with law-enforcement agencies, or selfish pressure groups of other kinds.

A legislature or Congress which becomes a mere recording machine of waves of feeling or organized pressures ceases to be a deliberative body. "Write your congressman" is good advice only if the writer has himself carefully deliberated the issue involved. It is more important to have a representative whose honesty and wisdom one can trust.

The American people could do much to create a more civilized atmosphere if they would more vigorously and publicly condemn campaigns of character assassination based on unsupported and irresponsible charges. Our libel laws are much looser than are those in Great Britain. It is practically impossible to win a suit for libel where one can prove no damages beyond an offense to one's honor. Almost any kind of slander goes on the floor of Congress under cover of congressional immunity. Certain journalists and radio commentators—some with a wide audience—have themselves so well insured against libel suits that they feel they can risk making charges that, in another age, would have brought a challenge to a duel. Indiscriminate mudslinging coarsens the whole tone and temper of the nation and increases general cynicism.

Democratic government will never survive the shocks of this epoch of change and overturn merely by its *theoretical* virtues. Democracy, to survive, must provide not only popular government, but *good* government. It must not only represent the people. It must represent in large measure the *best* in the people—the best in their traditions and in their character. It must preserve liberty without permitting liberty to degenerate into license, and maintain authority without permitting authority to degenerate into tyranny.

Such government requires certain dispositions of mind on the part of the governed: a high respect for law, a natural respect for oneself and others, and a willingness to subject issues to the tests of reason. It requires the presence of a natural nobility who set the tones and standards of society; not an aristocracy of birth, or of wealth, or of power groups, but an aristocracy of brains and virtue—persons who welcome and accept responsibility without hope of personal gain.

To increase the number of such persons is the function of democratic education. The majority of the American people undoubtedly put the national welfare above their own peculiar interests, yet this majority is never adequately represented. It never will be unless more people participate more actively in party life at the grass roots.

CONGRESS AGAINST SIN [8]

Public indignation at the revelations of the Fulbright and Kefauver committees has led to one of the most timely series of hearings to be held by a congressional body in recent years. A subcommittee of the Senate Committee on Labor and Public Welfare, under chairmanship of Senator Paul Douglas of Illinois, has been considering legislation to implement the Senate resolution adopted last March under the prodding of Senator Fulbright. The Fulbright resolution sought "to strengthen the faith and confidence of the American people in the government by assisting in the establishment of higher

[8] From an editorial in *Christian Century*. 68:910-11. August 8, 1951. Reprinted by permission.

moral standards in the official conduct of the executive and legislative branches of the government." . . .

Nothing very new or sensational has come out of the hearings before the Douglas committee. This committee has not been on the trail of more mink coats: the Fulbright committee did that job. Neither has it followed up the lead suggested by Senator Benton on the relation between government morals and campaign costs; that is being left to the Gillette committee which is soon to go into public action. (Senator Benton's statement that it cost two senators $2,000,000 apiece to be elected—$1,925,000 more than each will be paid during his term—attracted surprisingly little attention.) The Douglas committee may have sympathized with the contention of Comptroller General Warren that "cost plus" contracts covering military items are the greatest single source of corruption at Washington. But it is not expected to recommend legislation to end them. "Cost plus" is the gravy in which American big business is wallowing, and the senators know they haven't a chance in the world of putting an end to the practice.

But the Douglas committee, following the lead of the Fulbright resolution, is expected to recommend that some sort of permanent, nonpartisan commission be formed to act as a sort of continuing check on government morals. This would be made up of men and women whose standards of judgment would command respect. It would have a full-time staff to provide it with data. It would issue reports to the American public, probably once every two years. This same commission might be asked by Congress to formulate a code of ethics for government personnel, although Secretary of Commerce Sawyer, with White House approval, has told Senator Douglas that writing such a code would be a waste of time. Possibly it might be asked to suggest to other bodies effective ways for overhauling federal corrupt practices acts. . . .

If there are public servants who can be bribed, there have to be those who want to bribe them. As the pungent Harold Ickes reminded the committee, "Within my knowledge, no public officer has ever bribed himself." . . .

Here, whether or not Senator Douglas and his committee members are prepared to come to grips with it, is the core of their problem. For democratic government, self-government in any form, is a moral adventure. If self-restraint vanishes, if the subordination of self-interest to the larger good goes into the discard, then self-government will lose all moral authority and vigor. Eventually, it will collapse.

We are for commissions, codes or anything else Congress can employ to impress the seriousness of this moral situation and the need for constant concern on every part of the government and on the public. But the problem goes deeper than committee reports or the compilation of codes. It goes clear down to the decision as to whether we are simply adapting our acts to passing phases of manners and customs. It is on the rock of this latter belief—a belief fostered by schools and courts and all the voices of a secularistic society—that the moral integrity of our way of life is being shattered.

WHO CARES? [9]

Ten years ago, in July 1941, months before the attack on Pearl Harbor, the *Journal* published an editorial

[9] From editorial in the *Ladies' Home Journal.* 68:47. October 1951. Reprinted by special permission from the *Ladies' Home Journal.* Copyright, 1951. The Curtis Publishing Company.

—"That Freedom Shall Not Perish"—stating, among other things, that democracy was worth fighting for. In part, that editorial read:

> And the curious thing about democracy is this: a bad government can suppress it; a good government can permit and even encourage it; but democracy can flourish and grow strong only in the hearts and minds of a myriad of individual men.
>
> That is the strength of democracy and its weakness. It is a government of, by and for individuals. Democracy does not tell its citizens what to do. Its citizens tell a democracy what to do. If its citizens are strong and wise and self-sacrificing for a common ideal, democracy will succeed; if they are not it will fail, whether ground out by the iron heel of Hitler or smothered in a thousand internal strifes.
>
> In the difficult, terrible world of today, democracy—the only governmental system yet tried which respects the dignity of the individual man—democracy has no single chance, we believe, to endure, unless Americans—American men and women and children—have it stamped upon their spirits as an ideal for which they as individuals are ready to fight and, if need be, die; for which they as individuals are willing to do the even harder thing—live.

This, we believed then. In the great, confused war which followed, millions believed it so fiercely they were willing to die and did die for this belief. We who survived, if we still believe, must be willing now to fight on, day after day, for our belief. Are you willing?

Democracy is more than an abstract idea or an ideal. It does not float over us like a cloud. Definitions of democracy not stated in terms of its day-to-day operation are meaningless. The label "democracy" can be slapped onto all manner of nefarious schemes, including communist tyranny, by smooth-talking radio politicians—and you have heard it done. *Democracy is the free cooperation of a thinking and acting people.* Democracy is what each individual person actually *does* to contribute to his self-government. It has no other being. When a substantial number of us stop contributing—because of laziness, fear, or because we're just too busy making a living—democracy dies. . . .

Taking an active part in the political life of one's community, the "grass roots" of democracy, requires more than desultory effort from the "Gosh, what can I do?" citizen. It requires gritty persistence, sweat, and perhaps tears, if not blood. Blood our young men pour out—in Korea or elsewhere—when we fail to act, fail to do our part, seek to close our eyes to what must be done here and now.

The most radical—and the most successful—system of government ever devised by man is that system which permits people to govern themselves. "Government of, by and for the people" has always been a political system in peril. Seldom has it been in such peril, from inertia, as it is today. External threats to democracy exist—and we must be militarily prepared to meet them around the world—but democracy in the United States is in greater danger from its "do-nothing citizens" than from military attack. The practical application of "government by the people" has grown frighteningly close to "government by default" in these complacent United States.

There is no need to cite the appalling numbers of eligible voters who fail to vote in primary elections. Did you vote? Or, for that matter, who fail to vote in the most crucial presidential elections. Did you even vote in that? One out of two voters didn't. You should vote, but if you wait until election day to participate in self-government, it is almost too late. To do nothing more than vote is, in effect, to do very little. Not enough to survive. Failure to vote is one of few clear-cut examples of suicide by choice. No amount of complaining about the government can make up for your failure.

It is hard to understand how the exciting miracle of self-government—attained by the self-sacrifice of those in our Revolutionary and Civil wars who believed it was more precious than life itself—can be ignored, and even belittled, by so many of us who are privileged to exercise it. "Politics is a dirty business—let George do it" has become almost a national slogan. "George" is a cog in some "unbeatable" political machine. The man for whom George votes is the crook in office—though he may have to flee in disgrace when the heat is, temporarily, on. Pride of participation in our government has sunk to such a dismal low that it is socially acceptable for many to boast of their political indifference—"I am not now, and I never have been, a member of *any* political party!" This is the bitterest irony, and it is unhealthy in the most literal sense of the word.

Testifying before a Senate subcommittee on ethics in government, responsible and politically experienced citizens have said that we cannot have a higher standard in our politics unless we have it in our citizens. That's you. Unless our citizens care about graft and immorality in public life, graft and immorality will increase, because they make millions for the politically crooked—and the gamblers who buy them.

If you wait until voting time you will frequently only have a choice between two men of indifferent principles. These men were chosen because they promised to support a machine or a strong pressure group. They were chosen because they *do not intend* to govern as well as possible in the interest of all. At the present time it's more profitable to be crooked than honest, politically—and you pay the bill.

The problem of each citizen is this—to see that politics in his locality, his township, his election district, his county, is drawing in the best brains and effort of the most responsible citizens of his community, including himself. If that is done at the local level, it will be achieved at the national level. There is no way by which national politics can be more intelligent, more ethical, more courageous than the local groups in which it has its roots. That's why you, yes, you—can do something about it.

Democracy will not endure unless it is a good democracy. It can endure only if it is a fairminded government of fair and honest men, providing opportunities for the maximum educational, economic and social growth of each of its citizens—growth not only in economic standing, but also growth to man's fullest stature ethically (for democracy is essentially a spiritual and ethical conception, envisioning citizens strong and free and unafraid enough to care that their neighbors be also strong and free).

If democracy grows cynical and corrupt, it will perish—either to enemies without, or to powerminded men within. We are the only ones who can preserve it—all of us, as citizens.

TRUMAN MESSAGE ON REPORTING OFFICIALS' INCOMES [10]

To the Congress of the United States:

I recommend that the Congress enact legislation requiring officials in all branches of the government to

[10] Text of President Harry S. Truman's message to Congress, September 27, 1951. New York *Times*. p 12. September 28, 1951. Reprinted by permission.

place on the public record each year full information concerning their incomes from all sources, public and private. I believe this will be an important step in assuring the integrity of the public service and in protecting government officials against false and unfounded charges of improper conduct.

The overwhelming majority of the people who are working for the Federal Government in the legislative, judicial, and executive branches are decent, honest, and upright citizens who are doing their very best in the public interest. I believe that the standards of conduct now prevailing in the government service compare favorably with those of the past and with the standards now prevailing in business and the professions.

Nevertheless, it should be our constant aim to improve these standards. As the burdens of the government increase during this defense period, and more and more citizens enter into business or financial dealings with the government, it is particularly necessary to tighten up on our regulatory procedures, and to be sure that uniformly high legal and moral standards apply to all phases of the relationship between the citizen and his government.

In operations as large as those of our government today, with so much depending on official action in the Congress and in the executive agencies, there are bound to be attempts by private citizens or special interest groups to gain their ends by illegal or improper means.

Unfortunately, there are sometimes cases where members of the executive and legislative branches yield to the temptation to let their public acts be swayed by private interest. We must therefore be constantly on the alert to prevent illegal or improper conduct, and to discover and punish any instances of it that may occur.

We must also guard against the danger that the misconduct of a few will result in unwarranted suspicion and distrust of the honesty of all government officials.

In recent months, there has been something amounting to a deliberate effort to discredit the government services. Attempts have been made through implication and innuendo, and by exaggeration and distortion of the facts in a few cases, to create the impression that graft and corruption are running rampant through the whole government.

To my mind the most disturbing feature of the charges and rumors stirred up by these attempts is their effect on the confidence of the American people in their government and in all the individuals who make up the government.

I am told that people all around the country are getting a mistaken and a distorted impression that the government is full of evildoers, full of men and women with low standards of morality, full of people who are lining their own pockets and disregarding the public interest.

This is a terrible distortion of the true facts about our government. It would be tragic *if* our citizens came to believe it. It would be tragic for the American people themselves to have such an idea about their government, and it would be a terrible tragedy for all those who serve within the government. None of us can afford to let the whole body of public officials be given a bad name by accusations, rumors, and sensational publicity tending to smear everybody.

I believe the best thing we can do to spike this effort to discredit government officials is to place all the facts right on the record. The facts themselves are the best cure for public doubts and uncertainty.

I recommend, therefore, that the Congress promptly enact a statute which will require all full-time civilian presidential appointees, including members of the Federal bench; all elected officers of the Federal Government, including members of the Congress; and all other top officials and employees of the three branches of the government—say those receiving salaries of $10,000 or more, plus flag and general officers of the armed services—to file annually a statement of their total incomes, including amounts over and above their government salaries, and the sources of this outside income.

Consideration should also be given to requiring other government employees to file such statements if their outside income exceeds a specified amount—perhaps $1,000 a year.

Some items which are not ordinarily counted as income, such as gifts and loans, should be included in the statements filed under this statute. Penalties for willful violation of this statute should be equivalent to those for violation of the laws relating to the filing of income tax returns.

These statements when filed should be made accessible to the public.

Such public disclosure will, in my opinion, help to prevent illegal or improper conduct and at the same time protect government officers from unfounded suspicions.

The majority of Federal employees have no income of consequence other than their official salaries. Some of our best public servants, on the other hand, do have sizable amounts of outside income. The great public service that is being rendered today by many men who have been successful in business or other forms of endeavor demonstrates that no distinction can be drawn between these two groups in terms of the public good.

The disclosure of current outside income, however, will strike at the danger of gifts or other inducements made for the purpose of influencing official action, and at the danger of outside interests affecting public decisions.

A disclosure of all sources of outside income will be of obvious help in tracking down any case of wrongdoing. Furthermore, the mere existence of a requirement that such disclosure be made will act as a deterrent to improper conduct.

If an official of an executive agency knew that he would have to disclose the fact that he accepted a gift or loan from a private company with which he has public business, of if a member of Congress who is on a committee concerned with a certain industry knew that he would have to disclose the fact that he accepted a fee from a company in that industry, I believe the chances are that such gifts or fees would not be accepted.

Such a disclosure procedure will also serve to protect officials and legislators from widespread misunderstanding on the part of the public. Our citizens will be able to see for themselves that the talk about corruption and enrichment in public office is grossly exaggerated.

As a general rule, I do not like to see public officials, or any other particular group, subjected to rules and requirements which do not apply to the rest of the population. But at the same time, public office is a privilege, not a right. And people who accept the privilege of holding office in the government must of necessity expect that their entire conduct should be open to inspection by the people they are serving.

With all the questions that are being raised today about the probity and honesty of public officials, I think all of us should be prepared to place the facts about our income on the public record. We should be willing to do this in the public interest, if the requirement is applied equally and fairly to the officials of all three branches of our government.

This is the best protection we can give ourselves and all of our co-workers against the charge of widespread graft and favoritism in the public service.

I know of no other single step that will do so much good, so quickly, in protecting the reputations of our public servants and—at the same time—in producing concrete indications of any really questionable practices.

Much the same considerations apply also, I believe, to those people who hold the principal positions of responsibility in our great political parties. Of course, these offices are not government positions. But those who hold them are necessarily brought into very close contact with the government.

And our major political parties have traditionally been so much a part of our whole system of government, that those responsible for the conduct of party business are in fact, if not in law, charged with a real public responsibility.

For that reason, I would favor including the principal national party officials and employees among those persons required to file annual income statements along the lines I have described.

The legislation I have here recommended should be passed as soon as possible. If action cannot be completed before adjournment of the present session, then I earnestly hope that the Congress will finish the task as soon as it reconvenes. We should lose no time in placing all the facts before the country, and in clearing up those false impressions that are injurious to the proper functioning of our government.

I believe also that both the Congress and the Executive should continue to search for other means, legislative and administrative alike, to reassure the American people about the high standards of their government and to make sure that those high standards continue to be maintained by every individual who holds public office.

ETHICAL STANDARDS IN THE FEDERAL GOVERNMENT [11]

Ethics in government is a subject with almost endless ramifications. The standards of conduct of the legislative, executive, and judicial branches of government are interwoven. The standards of conduct of all these public servants also are interwoven with those of all who actively take part in public affairs, and of all who do business with the government. The morals of official conduct may be distinguished, but certainly not separated, from public morals generally. The moral standards of the country, indeed, provide the ethical environment which in turn conditions the standards of behavior of public officials. Low standards in the conduct of public affairs are a symptom of low standards in the country generally. High standards in the country are reflected in high standards in government.

But that is only half of the story. The relationship is not slavish, and there is a two-way action. The conduct of public officials is also a powerful example influencing the general public toward higher or lower standards.

Confucius, who was himself a high official, long ago pointed out that the example which the governor of a

[11] From report of special subcommittee (Paul H. Douglas, chairman) of the Senate Committee on Labor and Public Welfare. (Senate Committee Print, October 17, 1951) 82d Congress, 1st session. Supt. of Docs. Washington 25, D.C. 1951. p 1-5, 7-15.

province set was indeed far more important than his official acts. And what was true of the simple agricultural society of China centuries before the Christian era is even more true in our own more complex world today. The standards of the public will be raised if leaders in public life practice vigorous integrity. They will be lowered if these leaders are lax in their personal or official behavior.

This reciprocal relationship between the ethics of the public and ethics of public representatives was repeatedly emphasized in the testimony presented to the subcommittee. The nations's debt to the churches, the schools, and the homes, the great moral teachers, is clearly recognized. The morality of the state is only partly subject to its own control. The responsibility of religious and educational institutions and of parents is enormous.

There is some tendency on the part of public officials, however, to minimize their own role and their responsibility for leadership by example. American standards generally are high enough so that political leaders can insist on and get high standards of conduct in the government if they choose to do so, and go about it with vigor. . . .

The task of analyzing the problem fully must be left to the recommended Commission [see p 146]. Some aspects of American ethics which have been brought out in the testimony, however, should be noted. One of them is the simultaneous existence of conflicting codes of conduct.

Double standards are more prevalent than most men realize and are, perhaps, at the root of the problem of ethics in government. The free American society with its system of democratic and representative government is based upon some of the highest ideals of Jewish-Christian-Greek thought, and it could not have developed as it has without those basic ideals as a moving force in the life of successive generations. The man who sweareth to his own hurt and changeth not is essential in both the business and political worlds. In maintaining the effectiveness of an organization, the character of men in key positions is recognized to be as important as their intelligence. Americans venerate Washington for his integrity, and Lincoln for his unswerving dedication to the Union. These judgments reflect the enduring values of basic American ideals.

The accepted ideals are challenged daily, however, by contrary values. The clever man who makes a "fast buck" gets a certain amount of acclaim, provided he makes enough of them. The political trickster frequently can claim his rewards—if he wins. There is a tolerance in American life for unscrupulous methods which bring immediate rewards, even though those methods, if they should become universal, would destroy the very society in which they are tolerated.

Veneration for the principle of government according to law has its inverse side—an erroneous assumption that what is lawful is right. Although this is an untruth which authoritarian governments of all varieties have demonstrated vividly and recently, representative governments also must be on guard lest they make the same mistake. Where discretion exists in making law, the law itself is not a sufficient guide.

Example of double standards can be found in all walks of life today. The credit system of the country is based upon faithfulnes in meeting obligations, and banks are long-established fiduciary institutions. Yet some bankers have felt no compunctions about using RFC refinancing to rid themselves of bad risks. The businessman's code is to be independent and stand on his own feet, but some organized industries, as well as other economic groups, do not hesitate to use all possible force to secure highly favorable decisions from legislators and administrators at the public expense. A fair system of representation is a sacred element in the American political system, yet some politicians lightheartedly steal representation from the citizens of their own states by creating grossly disproportionate congressional districts, and from rival parties by gerrymandering boundaries. The same situation is often found in state legislative districts. The claim of Congress to moral authority is based upon its representative character, yet have not the two houses sometimes challenged the representative principle in their internal distribution of offices?

While we primarily deal in this report with the ethical problems of the national government, we should recognize that conditions in Washington and in government agencies are but the reflection of what also occurs on state and local levels, only in an aggravated form. If citizens who decry failures on the national level would take more interest in their local elections and in party organization, many of the sources of infection would be cleared up. Citizens cannot absolve themselves of responsibility because of their inaction and indeed their frequent connivance with low standards of ethics in all walks of life and all levels of government.

There is in American life a double standard, one highly responsible in its warm feeling for the welfare of our fellows, and the other coldly irresponsible in its single-minded devotion to direct personal advantage. The ruthless standard is epitomized by the traditional comment that "business is business" or "politics is politics." When the two realms of economics and politics are combined, however, there is a clear danger to society from aggressive and self-centered policies. If economic capacity and political power are combined and used indiscriminately for the personal gain of individuals, groups and classes, is there any assurance that America as we know it can survive? The greatest and most subtle danger is not a challenge to the Constitution or the law of the land, but it is a combining of forces to make public policies which may be completely constitutional and entirely legal but which are not in the interest of all the people.

In the past we have assumed that the aggressive forces in American life neutralized each other. That was the theory of Madison as expressed in the *Federalist*. That now seems doubtful at best. Sometimes, they reinforce each other. Even from the most egoistic point of view, there is no advantage in exploiting a system by means which will destroy it, yet older nations have not learned this lesson until too late, and it may be that the dangers of such exploitation tend always to be overlooked by the participants.

We should also realize that morality is violated not merely by politicians and by the weak, but also frequently by the strong and powerful, who sometimes are able to have their antisocial acts approved by legislation or court action. The medieval English quatrain about the way in which the common lands were enclosed and taken over by the nobility of England has also real meaning for our times:

> The law locks up both man and woman
> Who steals the goose from off the common,
> But lets the greater felon loose
> Who steals the common from the goose.

Witnesses called attention to other characteristics of American life which have a bearing upon ethical standards in public affairs and these views may be presented in the form of questions:

(1) Is there a secular trend in America which creates a new moral problem? Have the churches declined as a training ground for moral conduct? If such a trend exists and should continue, what will be the consequences?

(2) Do people have an overweening desire for wide social approval which makes them less independent in their judgments, less loyal to ancient values, and more inclined to go along with the sentiment or the practice of the moment?

(3) Are Americans as citizens and voters prone to be undiscriminating in their thinking? Do they lack the skepticism to reserve judgment until evidence is presented? Do they tend to lump together whole categories of people or situations without discriminating as to significant differences? If these traits of a politically immature people should be found to exist, would they indicate some degree of gullibility as to reckless charges, smear tactics, and emotionalism generally? Would they not raise some question as to the American capacity to deal realistically with complex issues and to avoid beguiling panaceas or wishful thinking?

(4) Is there a dominantly emotional outlook on public affairs and politics that leads to inconsistent attitudes and violent changes in opinion? Witnesses called attention to the extent of nonvoting and to a general apathy in regard to politics interrupted at times by intense interest and feverish reform. In the abstract, the public service is stereotyped in popular opinion as both lazily bureaucratic and unduly zealous, although these general

stereotypes are contradicted by quite favorable reactions to many public servants when considered as individuals, namely, school teachers, postmen, county agents, etc. Moods of optimism and pessimism come in rapid succession. Fears of scarcity are not quieted before fears of surplus appear. A sanguine mood in regard to international affairs gives way quickly to the fear of total war. Fluctuations in popular feeling seem to be much greater than can be explained by changes in the facts.

(5) Is there a general ignorance of the basic ethical and political ideas upon which American institutions were founded? Are Americans unaware of the ideas and principles which really control them today? If such ignorance exists, how does it affect capacity to deal with present-day problems of public affairs?

The subcommittee comes to no conclusion on these points, but the seriousness with which they are raised by wise and experienced men does indicate that they are questions of significance for which answers should be sought by a thorough inquiry.

In the Federal Government, the forces that would drive public servants from the straight and narrow path of virtue center chiefly upon a limited area, the area in which government is heavily "action-laden." This is the area in which there are big economic stakes, where the decisions of legislators and administrators directly affect the business, or the property, or the income of particular groups or individuals. The abuses of discretion or the exploitation of power are most serious chiefly where the government is dispensing valuable rights and privileges, constructing extensive public works, spending vast sums for military supplies and equipment, making loans, granting direct or indirect subsidies, levying taxes, and regulating the activities of privileged monopolies or economic practices in which there is a public interest.

In making policies to govern these functions, legislators have almost complete discretion, and for successful administration of these policies, administrators must also be given a large degree of discretion. Where such discretionary power exists, it can be abused or exploited. Institutional arrangements can narrow the risk, but not eliminate it. Neither can the functions be abandoned entirely. Although the area where integrity is most seriously threatened is a limited area, it is a crucial one, where reasonable and wise use of discretion in the public interest is imperative.

The overwhelming weight of testimony taken by the subcommittee is that the basic integrity of the Federal Government, in most branches, is relatively high. Most public servants, it was agreed, are honest and faithful. Witnesses with the longest experience in public affairs stated that standards of official conduct and public morals generally are rising although the existence of dips in this long-term trend was conceded. The general trend, also, does not preclude significant deviations in particular fields or at particular levels of activity.

We also believe that the ethical standards of public officials are probably higher than those prevailing in business and other walks of life. On this point, also, there was persuasive testimony from men of experience in both government and business and from observers of both. Public officials apparently are more conscious of the problem of moral standards. The resentment which public officials sometimes show when subjected to public criticism may be explained in part by their awareness of the fact that some of their critics would be even more vulnerable to criticism if the same standards were applied. Present conclusions, however, must be tentative and this is doubtless a situation which the [recommended] Commission on Ethics in Government will wish to investigate further.

There is nothing in the testimony, however, when considered as a whole, to make either the public or public servants complacent. No group in society is in a position to point the finger of scorn at others. Influence peddlers can exist only as long as businessmen or others are willing to patronize them. Favoritism can be a problem only when individual men and women seek favors of the government. Gifts, improper pressure, and bribes come from outside the government, from individuals, from organizations, and from groups which are part of what we call the "public." When educational institutions which we have long regarded as responsible for moral leadership are troubled with problems of professionalism, commercialism, and dishonesty in amateur athletics, it is evident that we are all living in the same glass house.

Standards of conduct seem high and rising when viewed against the background of fifty years ago. But we are living in the 1950's, not the 1890's, and the need for high standards of integrity, as well as competence, has grown even faster than the standards have risen. Conceivably, the country is falling behind in its ability to deal with the political and ethical problems of the day.

The subcommittee attempted to supplement, not to duplicate, the investigations of other Senate and House committees, and at this point, in taking stock of the situation, it is proper to take notice of the investigations by other committees.

Influence peddling is a phenomenon that cannot be ignored. It is perhaps exaggerated, and the gullible have been defrauded by men whose only influence was fictitious. But the disclosures of the subcommittee under Senator Hoey's chairmanship showed that there was fire behind the smoke. It is clear that influence peddling is so widely believed to exist that even the most professional practice of bona fide law firms in Washington tends to be tinged with the influence idea. It may be imaginary, but it helps to encourage the clients; and waiting for business has become obsolete for loyal and influential members of the administration who leave the government to hang up their shingles in Washington.

The growth of influence peddling—both the fiction and the reality (whatever the dimensions of the latter)—is the result of a number of causes: the enormous increase of governmental activity in the "dangerous area" (described above); the substitution of negotiations for competitive procedures in placing defense contracts; the exodus of higher civil servants and officials from the government while the political party under which they have worked for many years continues in charge of the administration; and the universal practice of members of the Congress who feel it necessary to intervene with administrative agencies in behalf of their constituents. Members of Congress and Washington attorneys are similar in one respect—they both must make it explicit that they are handling matters only on their merits and that they are not attempting to tip the scales of justice, if they wish to discourage the belief that influence exists.

The challenge to the integrity of government through the acceptance by public officials of gifts, favors, and lucrative employment from persons or organizations which seek favorable decisions from government agencies was amply demonstrated by the investigations of the subcommittee which dealt with the RFC under the chairmanship of Senator Fulbright and by later investigations under the direction of Senator Hoey. When public officials fail to show a fine sense of propriety as to what their high responsibility requires them to do in order to maintain complete objectivity and impartiality, subsequent faulty decisions inevitably become suspect. Public servants who exercise discretion in making or helping to make important decisions should take every possible step to make certain that they have no personal motives or interest in the decisions which they make. If they do not take this precaution, they deliberately expose themselves to charges of favoritism and bias. This necessity has not yet been fully recognized within all branches of the government, but it should be.

The penetration of organized crime into the American system of government through its ability to control American politics at the grass roots was demonstrated beyond all reasonable doubt by the Kefauver subcommittee. Those disclosures challenge the integrity of American politics at its base, the local community. They suggest that the failure to find a better way of financing necessary political activities on the part of Americans, who are known to be a resourceful people, can be attributed only to negligence and a failure to take politics seriously. This inference is perhaps the most damaging of all to the ethics of American society.

The investigations of the Maritime Commission by the House Committee on Expenditures emphasized the dangers which are inherent in a policy of discretionary subsidies handled by a regulatory commission, particularly by an agency which has for its sole clientele the industry which receives the subsidies. Although the situation was confused by apparent faulty structure, by lax management, and by a statute that was not entirely clear, the committee found an apparent tendency to use the administrative processes to fix a wished-for amount of subsidy rather than to determine, in a reasonable way, the proper amount of the subsidy. The perils of such a tendency are obvious.

The House Executive Expenditures Subcommittee headed by Congressman Hardy has also been investigating procurement practices of purchasing agents of automotive parts for the armed services. Already it has revealed unfortunate instances in Detroit and Toledo of highly questionable gratuities from government contractors. Charges of apparent favoritism and exorbitant prices will be examined when the subcommittee opens its hearings on the cost, profits, and sale contract figures of these parts producers. As we face the necessity of an unprecedented, peacetime expansion of the country's military power, and as defense appropriations rise to the $60 billion level, the Hardy committee's work makes it clear the opportunities for such unjust enrichment at the expense of the public treasury are more numerous than ever before.

Another series of disclosures have already involved collectors of internal revenue in New York, Boston, Detroit, St. Louis, and San Francisco. One indictment for alleged kick-backs in tax settlements, three removals from office by the President, numerous suspensions and resignations and a grand jury investigation indicate that some public officials and taxpayers are willing, for personal gain, to undermine the fairness with which tax laws are enforced. Recent hearings before the Investigations Subcommittee headed by Senator Hoey have implicated another group of internal revenue employees on a lower level in acceptance of gifts and outside employment. Beyond the dereliction of duty by individuals thus disclosed, it is clear that these practices weaken the essential public confidence in the fairness of the tax laws and their enforcement. If repeated, such cases may make more difficult the successful financing of the national defense and necessary nonmilitary programs of the government.

The advent of a new member—lobbying—in the ranks of big business was documented by the Buchanan committee of the House of Representatives. The evidence indicates that hundreds of millions of dollars are spent annually to influence both legislation and administration. The activities of pressure groups were once thought to be merely a segment of American politics. It would be more accurate, today, to say that the political parties themselves have become a segment of a much vaster system of pressure politics, a year-round business with an infinite variety of forms and almost unlimited funds. The changes in magnitudes and in the constancy, variety, and volume of pressures have created additional problems and dangers for public servants and have at the same time made the objectivity and integrity of the public service more essential. These pressures are at the heart of the problem of ethics in government.

In the light of these facts, the broad outline of which cannot be doubted no matter how much men may differ over the details, there is no cause for complacency, either as to the conduct of public servants, the ethical standards which prevail, or the moral climate of the country.

Unfortunately, a good deal of complacency exists. Administrators, who lament the imperfectibility of human nature and suggest that nothing can be done except to try to get better men in government, seem to be ignorant of the power of leadership to set and maintain high standards in an organization, and that there is a responsibility for leadership to do so. For a department head to avow "deep faith in the basic integrity . . . of my Department" is not very reassuring when he does so, after three or four important officials of his department were involved in serious improprieties which had come to public attention and where subsequently still more improprieties were revealed. A defensive view that "You can't legislate the Ten Commandments" overlooks the fact that wherever the Ten Commandments are held in high regard, legislative bodies have found it necessary to elaborate and enforce their basic principles. It is the function of a considerable part of the penal code to deal in more detail with matters which are specifically prohibited by the Ten Commandments. Every civilized people supplements its moral code with an extensive criminal code and with a vast body of civil law. Indeed, a major index of advancement in the scale of civilization is the extent to which a society enforces this code. Administrators must be on guard lest they become more anxious to defend the reputation of their administration than they are to make sure of its integrity.

On the record, we in Congress, must also seem unduly complacent. Neither house has acted vigorously to tighten its discipline in moral matters or to raise its ethical standards. In recent years, some members have been convicted of crime and sent to prison, but they have not been expelled. Neither house has been particularly diligent in searching out and punishing questionable conduct on the part of its members. It is hard for every institution to discipline itself, and Congress is no exception.

The public has been more outspoken. There is no doubt that the failure of some administrators and legislators to comply with decent standards of conduct has caused genuine distress among thoughtful people and has fostered cynicism among many others. This is the reaction of the general public. Among those better-organized special groups which are accustomed to press both legislators and administrators for favorable decisions, however, almost no recognized spokesman has yet come forward to say with equal conviction that pressure groups and aggressive interests have responsibilities as well as privileges. They speak up quickly in defense of the sacred right of petition, but they do not assert that they have a corresponding obligation of restraint. The legitimacy of lobbying is stoutly defended, although it is no longer challenged. But there is little evidence that the pressure groups concede that such a right carries with it an obligation to use only acceptable methods and tactics. Lobbying is a profession which has not yet felt the need of establishing a code to distinguish between proper and improper practices. In fact, some of the sharpest criticism of the ethics of administrators and legislators comes from groups which have shown the least scruple about their own methods.

Complacency over ethical standards is unfortunate. It is true that over a long period there has been progress, but has it been enough when measured by the need? There is little to justify the assumption that progress is automatic in the field of moral standards. Perhaps the country is living off its moral capital. The embarrassing deviations which have popped into view in the investigations that Congress has undertaken and in the revelations of the press are not the product of intensive inquiries or a search for misdeeds, and are, therefore, doubly significant as evidence of a possibly serious deficiency in American life. A thorough study by the Commission on Ethics in Government is needed to reveal more fully the nature and the dimensions of this problem. . . .

Summary of Recommendations

1. *A Commission on Ethics in Government.* A Commission on Ethics in Government should be established by joint resolution of Congress. The Commission's function should be twofold, the first to investigate and

report to the President and to the Congress on the moral standards of official conduct of officers and employees of the United States; the effect thereon of the moral standards in business and political activity of persons and groups doing business with the government or seeking to influence public policy and administration; and the moral standards generally prevailing in society which condition the conduct of public affairs or which affect the strength and unity of the nation. The Commission's inquiry should focus primarily on the legislative and executive branches, but should not exclude the administration of justice, federally supported activities of the states, and such ideas, attitudes, habits, practices, and standards of American society as are relevant to the Commission's functions.

The second function of the Commission should be to recommend measures to improve and maintain at a high level moral standards of official conduct in the Federal Government and of all persons who participate in or are responsible for the conduct of public affairs. It should be noted that the Commission would not be concerned with the morals of individuals—governmental personnel or private citizens—except as they are involved in the conduct of public affairs.

The Commission should consist of fifteen members, five appointed by the President, five by the President of the Senate (i.e., the Vice President), and five by the Speaker of the House. All members should be persons of recognized integrity, judgment, and experience in public or civic affairs. Of the members appointed by the President, two should be public employees, one a career civil servant holding a position not above GS-16 [base pay $12,000 a year], and one holding an office of higher rank. Of the members appointed by the President of the Senate and Speaker of the House, in each case two should be members of the respective legislative body of the appointing officer, one a Democrat and one a Republican.

The Commission should have power to hold hearings and secure testimony and evidence, authority to employ staff, and funds to carry on its work. It should have two years in which to complete its investigation and report, but should place its major recommendations before the President and Congress during the first session of the Eighty-third Congress. It should terminate thirty days after submitting its final report.

This recommendation is embodied in Senate Joint Resolution 107, which has been reported favorably by the Labor and Public Welfare Committee. . . .

2. *Amendments to the Administrative Procedure Act.* The Administrative Procedure Act should be amended to provide that the following practices shall be improper for Federal officials and employees and shall be grounds for summary dismissal from the Federal service:

(a) Engaging in any personal business transaction or private arrangement for personal profit which accrues from or is based upon the official position, authority, or confidential information of the official or employee.

(b) Accepting any valuable gift, favor, or service directly or indirectly from any person or organization with which the official or employee transacts business for the government.

(c) Discussing future employment outside the government with a person or organization with which there is pending official business.

(d) Divulging valuable commercial or economic information of a confidential character to unauthorized persons or releasing such information in advance of its authorized release date.

(e) Becoming unduly involved, for example, through frequent luncheons, dinners, parties, or other expensive social engagements with persons outside the government with whom they do official business.

The Administrative Procedure Act should be amended to prohibit Federal officials who participate in the making of loans, granting of subsidies, negotiation of contracts, fixing of rates, or the issuance of valuable permits or certificates from acting in any official transaction or decision which chiefly concerns a person or organization by which they have been employed previously in the preceding two years or with which they have a valuable economic interest. Any violation of this prohibition should be grounds for summary dismissal.

The Administrative Procedure Act should be further amended:

(a) To provide that former Federal officials and employees shall not appear before agencies in which they were formerly employed in cases which they previously handled or of which they had some direct knowledge as Federal officials or employees and that they shall not participate in the preparation of such cases.

(b) To provide that for a period of two years following their termination, Federal officials and employees of the ranks GS-15 [base pay $10,800 a year] and above who leave the Government shall not appear before the Federal agencies in which they were formerly employed as the representative of a person or organization doing business with the government.

The penalties of disbarment from practice before a Federal agency and of cancellation of contract in appropriate cases should be authorized to discourage those who would corrupt as well as those who allow themselves to be corrupted. Publicity for findings of improper practices would serve as a further deterrent. . . .

3. *Mandatory Disclosure of Income, Assets, and Certain Transactions.* Legislation should be enacted requiring all members of Congress, all Federal officials receiving a salary of $10,000 or more, or who are in positions of GS-15 and above, or of equivalent rank, and the principal officials of national political parties to disclose their incomes, assets, and all dealings in securities and commodities. The disclosures should be made by filing reports with the Comptroller General on forms provided by him to show income by source and amounts and to identify assets and show their value. These reports should be annual.

The revelation of such information will tend to deter individuals from accepting any income, holding any assets, or making any transactions which they believe are questionable. It will encourage public officials and political leaders to judge their own conduct with greater care. It will also provide for the public and for the great majority of such public servants and party officials whose actions and motives rise above personal considerations, the strong ground of truth on which to stand against unfair charges and innuendo. . . .

4. *Thorough Study of Proposed Changes in Criminal Law.* The laws governing conflicts of interest and bribery should be amended to correct inconsistencies, close loopholes, and extend their coverage. The proposed amendments, which the subcommittee recommends for thorough study by executive agencies and appropriate congressional committees . . ., would if enacted effect changes which can be made quickly and which are obviously needed. This action should not preclude a more exhaustive examination of the law governing illegal practices by the Commission on Ethics in Government and more extensive revision which the Commission may recommend.

5. *Creation of a Citizens' Organization to Work for Better Government on the National Level.* Congress should encourage private citizens to establish a nonpartisan, national citizens' organization to formulate suggestions and support affirmative programs for the improvement of government service. The successes of many reforms in local and national Government stem from the activity of well-organized citizens' groups. To win public understanding of the recommendations of a Commission on Ethics and to serve as an effective watchdog over the administration of approved measures, such a national organization can be a most effective force.

6. *Measures Meriting Additional Study and Consideration.* In addition, certain measures have been proposed which have merit, but which should be further studied before action is taken. They can appropriately be considered by the Commission recommended above, by other committees of the Congress, or by other authorities. Among these measures are the following:

(a) The proposal that a Court of Ethics be established to hear complaints regarding improper practices of public officials, and to investigate and make public reports. It has been suggested that such a court would consider carefully defined practices not subject to prosecution under criminal law or to other normal legal processes and not adequately remedied by the governmental body in which they occurred. The standards to be applied by the court would require careful formulation. It is proposed that this supplementary tribunal should consist of rotating panels of retired judges, administrators, officers of the armed forces, and former legislators drawn from a larger list of such persons appointed by the President, by and with the advice and consent of the Senate. Reports and recommendations following the hearings of complaints against government officials and members of Congress would be published in the *Federal Register* or *Congressional Record.* It is the objective of the proposal that the ordinary citizen have recourse to a simpler procedure to secure redress against improper practices of government officials which endanger his or the public's interest.

(b) Revision and extension of legislation governing corrupt practices in elections and lobbying. Some of these statutes were enacted a long time ago; they were no more than first steps, which have not been followed up.

(c) Provision of public financial assistance for candidates in election campaigns.

(d) Action by particular functional or professional groups, both in the public service and outside of it, to formulate and adopt ethical codes governing their conduct of or participation in public affairs. Cooperation between such groups and the recommended Commission would be desirable. Among the groups within the Federal Service for which codes might well be prepared are members and ranking staff of regulatory commissions, other regulatory officials, contracting officers, procurement officers, personnel officers, responsible officials of lending agencies, and officials who handle subsidies, tax amortization certificates, and other valuable privileges.

(e) Vigorous enforcement of existing standards of conduct in public affairs whether contained in written or unwritten codes, so that known infractions by a few will not dishonor an entire body of public servants, most of whom are devoted and faithful. Logically this would include both reasonable adherence to the basic ideals of representative government in qualifying for and serving within the houses of Congress and consistent discipline within the administration covering ethical as well as political misconduct. Failure to adhere to the high standards which the public has a right to expect of public servants puts a stigma on the entire group when it goes undisciplined by those who are in authority.

(*f*) More general and determined efforts to recognize and reward high standards of conduct throughout the field of public affairs. In many instances, nothing more may be required than the sincere public recognition by responsible officials or political leaders. It is as necessary to recognize the desirable as it is to identify the undesirable.

(*g*) Strengthening of the Federal personnel policy and personnel system.

(*h*) Improved management in executive departments and agencies.

(*i*) Clarification by law of public policies so that their intent and effect will be clear, and so that administrators will have firm principles with which to guide the discretion vested in them. Subsidies should stand on their merits and not be hidden in other payments. Similarly, accounting practices should show the cost of government services or benefits to particular groups.

(*j*) Improvement of legislative-administrative relationships by consideration of Senator Kefauver's proposal (S. Res. 190) for a weekly or biweekly period in the Senate for questioning selected department heads.

(*k*) Assertion of the rule of fair play in debates on the floor of the House and Senate. Administrative officials attacked on the floor of either house should, under the rules, have protection equal to that afforded members of the house; and agency heads who are subject to personal attack on the floor should be given an opportunity to make an immediate or early reply in the same forum. Private citizens who are similarly attacked should have the right to reply at moderate length in the *Congressional Record.*

(*l*) The principle of fair procedures is as imperative in the legislative as in the administrative and judicial processes. The Standing Rules of the Senate and House of Representatives should provide for fair procedure in the investigating activities of committees.

WHAT WOMEN DID IN GARY [12]

This is the story of the murder of an innocent woman.

This is the story of a town so enmeshed by gambling syndicates and petty criminals that many officials, from the top down to the smallest public officer, were often willingly or helplessly incriminated.

This is the story of women, so determined to make their town a decent place to live in that they risked the threats of the underworld to their homes and children, to work, undeterred, for good government.

The story begins in Gary, Indiana, on the night of March 3, 1949. Mary Cheever, a popular and much respected teacher in one of Gary's high schools, was on her way home from a Parent-Teachers meeting, where she had been the principal speaker. A purse snatcher accosted Miss Cheever just outside her own apartment building, shot her at close range, and left her dead—not more than twelve feet from one of the main streets of Gary.

Mary Cheever's death was the culmination of a series of shocking crimes in Gary. During the previous two months of 1949, the town had experienced one murder every nine days, and any number of petty thefts and crimes. Gary had one of the worst traffic records in the

[12] From an article in *Ladies' Home Journal.* 68:51+. October 1951. Reprinted by special permission from the *Ladies' Home Journal.* Copyright, 1951. The Curtis Publishing Company.

United States. Gambling was one of the big businesses of the city. Gary had been cited by some authorities as the second crime center in the country, and by the American Social Hygiene Association as the nation's worst offender for open prostitution.

"Mary Cheever's death was the spark we needed," explains Mrs. Frank H. Collins, former president of Gary's Council of Social Agencies. "At the time we thought her death was utterly meaningless, a useless tragedy. Now we believe it was a symbol, calling us to action. We knew, then, that something had to be done."

The women of Gary went to work. Within four days of Miss Cheever's murder, they formed the Women's Citizens Committee, pledged to fight until Gary became a community where honest officials and efficient law enforcement were the rule and not the exception.

It is now more than two years since Mary Cheever's death. The racketeers who sneaked out of town for a few days to let the women get tired of trying to clean up Gary did come back. But they found the easy pickings to which they were accustomed had vanished. Their movements were followed at every turn by housewives and schoolteachers one would have thought too timid to meddle in the affairs of a vice syndicate. There isn't a brothel open in the whole town. There is a new prosecuting attorney who sees that offenders are quickly brought into court and punished to the full extent of the law. The lights are brighter at night, and you can walk down the streets after dark with safety. The job isn't done, by any means. The women are the first to tell you so. . . .

Miss Mary Cheever was buried Monday afternoon, March 7, 1949. That night two thousand women, called by a handful of leaders of various women's organizations, met in Seaman's Hall. Filled with righteous indignation as they listened to demands for law enforcement, the women in one accord leaped to their feet to march the three long blocks to City Hall where city council was in night session.

An ultimatum was read to Mayor Eugene Swartz and the city council:

The women of the city of Gary long have suffered from lack of police protection in their homes and on the streets; they have endured the humiliating and unsavory reputation of their home town spread across pages of national magazines. They have watched helplessly as neighbors and friends have been attacked on the streets and robbed in their homes and automobiles, with no aid from the law-enforcement division of the city government.

Citing Gary's flagrant record, they demanded that the superintendent of the Indiana State Police, Arthur M. Thurston, be called in immediately to survey the situation and make recommendations. They gave the mayor two weeks for action. Then, they said, "If the city government does not clean up the city, give it protection and make it safe for the citizens and their families, the women can and will, with God's help!"

It was Hylda Burton, a schoolteacher, who suggested that first night of the indignation meeting, "I move that this group be made a permanent organization, called the Women's Citizens Committee, and that the women who called us together be appointed on an advisory board."

"Our organization was really as simple as that at first," Beryl Ann Brownell, serious-minded young women's page editor of the Gary *Post-Tribune,* remembers. "We had no definite plans. We were simply united by the desire to clean up Gary."

Two weeks after their first visit to the City Hall, the Women's Citizens Committee marched again to see Mayor Swartz. He said he had done what he could to clamp down on gambling and prostitution. He refused the police-department shake-up the women demanded. He denied the existence of syndicated gambling. "We'll take this to the governor," the women said. And they did. . . .

By midsummer of 1949, Mayor Swartz assured the Women's Citizens Committee, "There's no open gambling or prostitution here now." After a conference with and encouragement from Captain Billick [a police officer appointed by Mayor Swartz as a special investigator of vice], the women decided on action which would focus the attention of the whole town on the illegal traffic going on right under the nose of the public. Then followed the famous two days when 160 women, representing as many different organizations (all members of the Women's Citizens Committee), "picketed" eighteen of the worst taverns, brothels, gambling houses. . . .

Poll watching was another step taken by the Women's Citizens Committee to insure better government. "We are convinced there were many irregularities at the polls, and although we couldn't take any direct action, we could prevent overt cheating," Mrs. Collins says. "In one precinct during our first observations, over half the voters had to be assisted. In each case we insisted that both a Republican and a Democrat judge be called in." Since poll watching has been practiced, she believes there has been steady improvement in voting practics. . . .

The women enlisted the help of men in Gary they knew were as eager to clean up the town as were they. The Gary Crime Commission was formed, dedicated to ferreting out proof of the tie-up between vice and local officeholders.

Bernard Spong, pastor of the Bethlehem Lutheran Church in Gary, is chairman of the commission. "The Crime Commission is really the 'baby' of the Women's

Citizens Committee. Our board is made up of fifteen men, twenty-one women, the latter from the Women's Citizens Committee. This gives the ladies the controlling vote in any controversial decision. They trust us," and he smiles, "but they want to be sure we do what they think best. Actually, the two groups work very closely together, and it is the women who keep us alive!" (The WCC's recent protest over the withholding of a grand-jury report on a probe in Lake County led the Senate Crime Committee to ask Criminal Court Judge William J. Murray for an explanation.)

With typical directness, when funds were needed to finance expert advice to the two organizations and for the dissemination of information to the public, the women simply started ringing doorbells. Within six weeks the Women's Citizens Committee treasury boasted $15,000, received in amounts ranging from $1 to $25. "One dollar made you a member of the WCC for two years. We soon had nine thousand members. And other people contributed to the cause because they agreed with us," they explain. . . .

Beginning as political novices, the leaders of the WCC had to learn through mistakes and hard work what they lacked in experience. "We were so sincere in our purpose, so sure our ends were right, we barged in any place. Once we interrupted the governor at a private luncheon to ask how he was proceeding in the investigation of Gary," Mrs. Saks smiles in recollection. Their work paid dividends, however, when, for example, the state legislature recently passed overwhelmingly two bills their organization had sponsored. The first provided for four special investigators in Lake County to assist the prosecuting attorney search out law violators; the second was designed to reduce by half the number of taverns in Lake County. "Ours was the only county in the state which could legally have one tavern to every five hundred people," the Reverend Mr. Spong declares. "And Gary had many more than that."

Each member of the Women's Citizens Committee advisory board approaches her work with serious spiritual dedication. "We begin each meeting with prayer," they say. The clergy of Gary, Catholic and Protestant, were quick to encourage their work.

Although the birth of the Women's Citizens Committee was almost spontaneous, its development has been carefully nurtured. The eighteen-member advisory board, which serves for two years, is the executive body of the organization. Thus far there has never been a permanent chairman, and members of the board take turns holding this post for two-week periods. Representatives of more than 300 different women's groups in Gary act as a steering committee for the group, meeting on call to vote on major decisions. Individual members now number 18,000 of the ultimate goal of 25,000 women.

The women who have worked faithfully with the WCC since its inception represent a good cross section of the civic-minded in the city. There are white-haired, gentle Mrs. Frank H. Collins, long a worker in Catholic organizations, who remembers that during that first year, "I never had time to iron my husband's shirts—the phone was always ringing"; diminutive Marian Iams, a graduate of the University of Chicago, who continued to work in spite of the fact that . . . [the machine politicians] tried to disbar her husband after . . . [a] recording machine was traced to his office; Beryl Ann Brownell, whose reporting of the WCC's activities won for her in 1950 the title of "Woman Who Has Contributed Most to Journalism in Indiana"; eloquent Mrs. Benjamin Saks, who had worked with the Jewish women's organization, Hadassah, and has intimidated many an oily politician with her ability to "think on her feet"; fiery little Peg Griffith, who once laughed into the phone when a lisping thug warned her to "Lay off, thithter, it won't work"; Mrs. Catherine Johns, veteran principal of the Jefferson School, who has taught in Gary since 1907; Mary Jessee, trust officer at Gary National Bank; and Mrs. William P. Swan, a Negro, whose husband is principal of a Gary school. . . .

In a recent bulletin written by their pro tem chairman, WCC members were warned, "The people who don't want good government would be happy to have us all go back to our knitting. Will you make them happy? Or will you continue to work for a Gary you can be proud to call your home?"

The answer, it would appear, will bring no cheer to enemies of Gary's cleanup campaign.

IT'S TIME WOMEN TOOK DIRECT ACTION [13]

Shocked by revelations of corruption and moral callousness in public life, challenged by communism to prove that free government can work, the United States enters an election year facing a real crisis.

What can American women do about it? Why have American women not brought about higher standards of civic action long since? The answer is perfectly self-evident: American women through their powerful and valuable organizations have largely worked outside the apparatus of American politics and government. They have been bringing external pressure on government. Not enough of them have been working from inside,

[13] From an article by Erwin D. Canham, Editor, *Christian Science Monitor*. *Ladies' Home Journal*. 69:48+. January 1952. Reprinted by special permission from the *Ladies' Home Journal*. Copyright, 1952. The Curtis Publishing Company.

beginning at the lowest precinct levels, actually operating government. . . .

This is not to belittle the work of women's private organizations. They are performing prodigies of public betterment throughout the country. Their work is essential, and it deserves the highest praise. The League of Women Voters is a marvel of organization and energy. The "Build a Better Community" contest of the General Federation of Women's Clubs brought to light a magnificent range of achievement. The Business and Professional Women's Club is a civic dynamo from coast to coast. The Women's forums, local coordinations of existing organizations, are vital forces. The Women's Joint Congressional Committee is a powerful influence in Washington. And there are many others.

All these great good works should continue. But they bear somewhat the same relation to our political problems as the men's service clubs or, perhaps, the special-interest groups. They are not organic. They are unavoidably interested in their own corporate being. They have a proper vested interest in keeping their own organization going, in promoting its special achievements.

The problem is more direct than that. One experienced politician says that if he had about twelve reasonably intelligent, disinterested and faithful women regularly attending all township meetings in his county, the whole standard of honesty, selection of candidates, voting and performance would be on an entirely higher level.

There are women well able to fill these specifications in every precinct in the nation. And in many places, such women are already putting more time than that into civic programs. But nearly everywhere, these women are external to the political apparatus. They get excellent specific results whenever their political power rises to a critical mass. But their work concerns effects. It rarely becomes operational.

The whole situation is illustrated very well in the work of the League of Women Voters, of which I am a great admirer. The league is incredibly busy. At election year, it will address pertinent questions to the candidates and publicize their answers or evasions. It will get people to register, and to vote. It makes a big impact, it follows through. It is excellent, and none of it ought to be stopped. But it isn't direct political action. It is an educational process, or a lobbying technique, but it is not governing. The very same women might be exerting their pressure from the inside, starting with the precinct or the township, and sometimes they do. But I suspect that they would get twice as many results from the same foot-pounds of energy if they were inside the system.

In an increasing number of communities, of course, American women are getting directly into political work. Many of them came in through their activity in women's organizations. . . .

Once before in American history women had to make a transition from indirect to direct action. When they did it, they brought about an economic revolution. Up to a century ago, as Mary H. Donlon, chairman of the New York State Workmen's Compensation Board, points out in *Independent Woman,* organ of the National Federation of Business and Professional Women's Clubs, men did most of the retail buying. They took their products off to market, and the women had to take what they brought home. Doubtless the influence of the women was very great, but it was not direct. Then, beginning in about 1850, women started to take over the retail purchasing. By now they dominate it, and as a result, styles and standards and the whole scale of family living have been revolutionized. Women came into retail purchasing at the ground floor—the precinct level. They soon showed themselves to be shrewd, realistic, farsighted. There is nothing in the economic system to outrank the woman shopper.

What would happen if women moved into local politics as direct participants, just as they moved into retail purchasing? Can anyone doubt that the results would be just as revolutionary? Women would shop for political integrity just as effectively as they shop for durable yard goods and harmonious design. Women are said to be sentimental, thank goodness, but how often do their emotions run away with them in the grocery store or the department store? Not very often. Merchants have found no substitute for quality with the woman shopper. They know they have to guarantee satisfaction, or the penalty is swift and ruthless. They will lose the customer—perhaps many customers.

Women have seen in recent months what shoddy goods have crept onto the counters of American politics. The time to demand and obtain quality has come. The moment for direct action is here. During these very weeks, all the groundwork is being laid for . . . [the 1952] presidential elections. Women can have a great influence on the selection of delegates to the national conventions. But, far more important, women can get right now into the precinct and township work which will produce good local government. Out of that process, good state and good national government can flow.

The struggle for freedom in the world may well be waged and won, first of all, in the proof—or lack of it—of operative democracy provided in the American community. The battle against totalitarianism and the police state is not far off. It is here at home, where we have to make free government work well as an example for the undecided and unsatisfied millions elsewhere in the world. In this battle here at home, women can achieve what is nearest to their hearts: a safe and a free country in which their children can grow up. That means a free world. There is no other sound basis for world leadership.

TO MAKE YOUR VOTE COUNT [14]

When Mrs. E. A. Rendall, of Brownsville, Texas, found that the city's garbage ordinance was not being enforced even in the face of a threatened polio epidemic, she became a "political pilgrim." She got the League of Women Voters to organize the "Alley Annies," who patrolled the town, noted violations, checked police records and court blotters. Results: citizens' groups were formed, metal garbage containers appeared, the number of disposal trucks doubled. Now there's strict enforcement. Mrs. Rendall gave the *Ladies' Home Journal* her "tried and true" methods:

1. Get the facts. So armed, even the most timid woman gains courage. Politicians and officials cannot laugh her off, postpone or stall.

2. Know your town government. Know also who your officials are and the duties of each. Take your problem to the right department and directly to the person in charge. You will save time, gain the attention and respect due the person who knows what she wants and where to go.

3. Attend meetings of the city or county council, the local school board, other public agencies. Sit in a prominent place and take notes. Don't interrupt during the meeting, but ask any questions you have when the meeting is over.

[14] From an article by Margaret Hickey, Editor, Public Affairs Department, *Ladies' Home Journal*. *Ladies' Home Journal*. 69:48. January 1952. Reprinted by special permission from the *Ladies' Home Journal*. Copyright, 1952. The Curtis Publishing Company.

4. Examine the public records. Few women realize they are available — city charter, financial statements, budgets, payrolls, health reports, vital statistics. Officials may be reluctant, but they won't refuse them and will often furnish copies.

5. Learn about candidates for public office. But don't stop there—know your officials, elected and appointed. Follow them through their entire terms of office. Watch those they employ and those they appoint to boards, commissions, committees.

6. Know your election laws. All your efforts are wasted if voting practices are corrupt, so your work is not done until clean elections are assured. Ask to serve as an election official or a watcher at the polls. Even as a private citizen you can report to the election officials or board any violations you witness at the polls. If corrections are not made promptly you can take your complaint to the grand jury. Too few citizens exercise this right.

7. Talk, Talk, Talk. About what you see. What you read. About what happens at the meetings you attend. Over the back fence, at the grocery store, across the canasta table, talk about the facts of government, the issues and the candidates. Elections are won or lost by what people think and say. Have your say and cast your vote.

MORALITY IN PUBLIC LIFE [15]

Many people have assumed, once the title of this talk was announced, that this was to be the "holier than thou" part of the program. It would be very natural.

[15] From speech by Alistair Cooke, Chief United States Correspondent, *Manchester Guardian*, delivered at the New York *Herald Tribune* Forum, New York, October 22, 1951. *Vital Speeches of the Day.* 18:80-2. November 15, 1951. Reprinted by permission. (Mr. Cooke has been an American citizen since 1941.)

For Englishmen usually leave Washington with the compliment that Congress is not, and seems to have no intentions of becoming, the House of Commons. I spend some part of every year begging British and French journalists to start their study of American government not in Washington but in the places the men in Washington come from; so they may understand why a man from the goat country of Texas, west central Texas, keeps up such a lively interest in mohair and army uniforms, and why a man from California seems to have nothing on his mind but water, unless it is the oil that flows under it.

By such little expeditions it is possible for a foreigner to learn at the start one of the great differences between a congressman and a member of Parliament, and a difference which has everything to do with our theme tonight.

When a man goes to Westminster, he does not go as a one-man delegation from an industry or a crop. . . . Very often he may have only a rough idea of what his constituents do for a living. For there is no locality rule in the British system, which is not an oversight but a provision meant to leave the member of Parliament comparatively free to give his best to the affairs that concern the nation as a whole. This is quite different from watching the Congress bring up a bill and expecting your man to amend it in your interest.

The difference may not be so good for the folks back home—which could be a serious defect—but it does make possible a national legislature and encourages the honesty of its members. In his turn, the member is not pressed with lobbyists because he can have little say in framing legislation, since in the British system legislation is initiated in the Cabinet. This is not to say the Cabinet has an absolute power to make the laws. The standing committees do a good deal of drafting and amending; but they have two striking characteristics that distinguish them from the committees of Congress. They do not specialize in agriculture or banking or military affairs or any other subject. And their chairmen do not sit until they die. They are chosen, in no predictable order, by the Speaker of the House from a panel of names he has in his pocket.

These customs make it impossible to know in advance who will be studying what sort of legislation. And thus, also, Parliament is spared the heart-burning that afflicts us all in every new Congress when it appears that the chairman of some committee, whose bias we dislike is, alas, still in the land of the living.

These brief comparisons, you will already suspect, seem to be in the British favor, but you invited me to make them, and we chose a field distinct from antitrust legislation or domestic plumbing—in which the British have something to offer.

But it would be wrong to moon over the superior virtue of the British. Their human nature is much the same as ours—outside their own country sometimes more so—and their present ethical standards in government are something quite new.

In the eighteenth century parliamentary corruption was prodigious. In the nineteenth century, two events came along to change the public status of the House of Commons. One was the industrial revolution, which brought the new merchant class into opposition against a landed aristocracy, and soon made each side eager to set up rules to check the corruption of the other. The other event was Queen Victoria. The example of her piety depressed the English sinner for sixty hopeless years and added a new commandment to the decalogue: "Thou shall not be found out." This is not, of course, the same as virtue, but it is good propaganda for it and made all officers of government get the habit of being incorruptible in public. And the British people got so used to assuming that their legislators were honest that they were all the more shocked when any of them turned out to be frail.

In this period, too, the British had to invent a tradition to dignify their growing empire overseas and at the same time give idealistic young men a good reason to want to work for it. The tradition they invented was that of "the gentleman." Now in its decline, it is an easy tradition to make fun of, and one young English cynic has defined the mark of a gentleman as "utter grossness of soul tempered by a desire to behave nicely."

Well, we are all gross, but it is something to get a whole nation to believe that good behavior is the rule, and this ideal percolated through three generations, down all the social strata and produced a change in the British character so astonishing that the British now expect their King to be respectable and dutiful, their Parliament and Civil Service to be incorruptible, and their neighbor to be polite.

By the beginning of this century, certainly, the Parliament had acquired a pride in its public reputation so strong that in the last forty years there have been only about eight or more cases of what the British choose to define as corruption. They include such things as investigating four members of the government who were buying stock overseas while the government was negotiating for the product; a simple, old-fashioned case of embezzling by a member of Parliament in which, it is worth noting, the man was brought from prison after his conviction to the bar of the House and solemnly and ceremonially expelled from the House of Commons. They include the dilemma of a member of Parliament of eight years' standing who could not leave the House during a debate. He needed some important papers and so committed the unspeakable crime of sending his wife home on his own nontransferable railroad ticket. He was fined by the police court and allowed to resign from the House of Commons.

Fifteen years ago, a Cabinet minister leaked to a friend the news of a Cabinet decision to increase the tax on tea, and the friend took out covering insurance. The minister gained nothing at all from this indiscretion but he had to quit the House altogether and was never heard of again until he died.

Only a year or two ago the Chancellor of the Exchequer, going into the House to read his budget message, jokingly remarked to a newspaperman that it might still be possible to smoke and drink a glass of beer. The man telephoned his paper and Mr. Dalton resigned. He did so, like the other minister, not because of any law or rule but—as one of them said—"in honorable obedience to a broader constitution."

Even in the rarer cases of indiscretion in the Civil Service, the Board of Inquiry does not need to discover anything so blunt as a crime. It is enough if it finds that an official seems "to lack the instinct and perception by which the conduct of a Civil Service should be regulated."

This test, I must admit, is a rather mystical thing to use as a guide for our own government. But the British did not come to rely on a code until it was braced by good rules. Over eighty years ago, Parliament decided that election abuses were too passionate a subject to be left to Senate—I'm sorry, I mean parliamentary—investigation. It turned such things over to the courts, on the petition of a candidate with a grievance.

And it is a convention of the House of Commons that a member must publicly announce his financial interest in any subject in which he means to join in debate. And every member of a standing committee has to sign a declaration—a declaration of independence that would cause quite a stir in Washington. It says: "I swear that my constituents have no local interest in the bill and I have no personal interest in it."

From this very sketchy account, you will see that the member of Parliament is protected from his worst self by the system, whereas some other systems tend to put a representative on the receiving end of a cornucopia and then expect him to be a demigod.

What can we do to improve the system? This, I think, is what we have to ask, for the tendency in such debates as these is to fall back on righteous indignation, which does not really cure the absurdity of politicians in Boston and Philadelphia wringing their hands over the human clay of politicians in Chicago and Kansas City, until after another election the vice is versaed. All such moral gymnastics do nothing but turn the old rascals out and put the new rascals in.

I shall go at once, then, into a few suggestions and I make them not as a British correspondent but as an American citizen. I should think the first thing would be to expand greatly the Civil Service and make an immense increase in its whole pay scale, so that in our society a civil servant shall have a prestige at least as honorable as that of a successful manufacturer of candy or toothpaste. We might grow bold enough sometimes to suggest that we gather into the Civil Service all those jobs which are now at the disposal of the presidential pork barrel.

Next, I would take the investigation of election frauds out of the hands of Congress. And while we are at it, we might ask ourselves if we cannot drastically reform the scope of Senate investigations—of those which are made like inquests, anyway—for they ought to lead to action but now tend to amass so much evidence that nothing is done, party feeling is given a public message, and so much is said on both sides that the public after two million words of testimony can keep its preconceptions intact.

Finally, some wealthy foundation might well atone for its ancient sins by making a study of the connection between business and government. I believe with Mr. Dooley that no congressman ever corrupted himself, but as long as he is half representative and half business agent or trade delegate, business will too often be able to call the tune of the lawmaker.

And so long as we in our own lives observe two codes of conduct—a flexible code of ethics for business and self-righteous code for government officials—we shall go on getting congressmen and state and city officials who look awful until we discover that they are only the mirror-image of ourselves. For we suffer just now from a tug of war between the theory and the practice of American life. We believe in patriotism and unselfish public service, but we imbue our children with the idea that material success is the real goal. Our children consequently live in a puzzled shadow between our ideals and our habits. We tell them that no democracy is so precious to its people as ours, but whereas 90 per cent of the benighted Germans, 80 per cent of the Italians and 84 per cent of the British go to the polls, and in Australia you are fined if you stay away—only one qualified American in two bothers to vote. In our propaganda abroad, we tell our hard-pinched allies of Europe that we built a nation on an idea, but we point with more honest pride to our comforts.

Perhaps before we begin to reform the Congress, we might all begin humbly with our children and teach them in their teens that they get the sort of government they deserve; that grooming and clothes and a glittering kitchen are delightful things but are not necessarily the best of what history will remember America by. Let us tell them—and ourselves—that we can keep the hydramatic drive and still lose our democracy.

BIBLIOGRAPHY

An asterisk (*) preceding a reference indicates that the article or a part of it has been reprinted in this book.

Books, Pamphlets, and Documents

Allen, R. S. Our sovereign state. 413p. Vanguard Press. New York. '49.

Beasley, Norman. Politics has no morals. 229p. Charles Scribner's Sons. New York. '49.

Bolles, E. B. How to get rich in Washington; rich man's division of the welfare state. 309p. W. W. Norton & Co. New York. '52.

*Chase, Stuart. Democracy under pressure. 142p. Twentieth Century Fund. New York 18. '45.

Connell, F. J. Morality and government. 38p. National Council of Catholic Men. 1312 Massachusetts Ave. Washington 6, D.C. '49.

Frank, L. K. Society as the patient. 395p. Rutgers University Press. New Brunswick, N.J. '48.

*Herring, Pendleton. Public administration and the public interest. 416p. McGraw-Hill Book Co. New York. '36.

Hillenbrand, M. J. Power and morals. 217p. Columbia University Press. New York. '49.

King, W. J. Moral aspects of dishonesty in public office. 221p. Catholic University of America Press. Washington, D.C. '49.

Sellin, Thorsten. Culture conflict and crime. 116p. (Bulletin 41) Social Science Research Council. New York. '38.

Stoker, Charles. Thicker'n thieves. 415p. Sutter & Co. 406 Wilshire Blvd. Santa Monica, Calif. '51.

*United States. Senate. Committee on Labor and Public Welfare. Ethical standards in the Federal Government; report of special subcommittee (Paul H. Douglas, chairman). (Senate Committee Print, October 17, 1951) 89p. 82d Congress, 1st session. Supt. of Docs. Washington 25, D.C. '51.

United States. Senate. Special Committee to Investigate Organized Crime in Interstate Commerce. Final report (S. Report no725) 104p. 82d Congress, 1st session. Supt. of Docs. Washington 25, D.C. '51.
Kefauver committee report.

Wallas, Graham. Human nature in politics. 4th ed. 301p. Macmillan Co. New York. '50.

Wilson, H. H. Congress: corruption and compromise. 337p. Rinehart & Co. New York. '51.

PERIODICALS

American Economic Review. 34:sup41-7. Mr. '44. Ethics in the study of democratic politics. F. G. Wilson.

American Mercury. 58:539-46. My. '44. Mailed fist in Tennessee. C. W. Van Devander.

American Mercury. 59:408-15. O. '44. O'Connell's machine in Albany. C. W. Van Devander.

American Mercury. 68:435-47. Ap. '49. Huey Long's Louisiana hayride. Hodding Carter.

American Political Science Review. 43:1119-44. D. '49. Administrative ethics and the rule of law. F. M. Marx.

American Scholar. 18, no2:207-16. [Ap.] '49. American Scholar forum; national interest and moral principles in foreign policy. H. J. Morgenthau; W. T. R. Fox.

*Annals of the American Academy of Political and Social Science. 189:17-21. Ja. '37. Spoils and the racket. T. J. Haggerty.

Annals of the American Academy of Political and Social Science. 259:30-45. S. '48. Precinct workers. Sonya Forthal.

Atlantic Monthly. 135:742-8. Je. '25. Direct primary: a study from life. I. B. Oakley.

Atlantic Monthly. 173:92-5. Ap. '44. Leaven of conscience. Jacques Maritain.

Atlantic Monthly. 180:21-4. Jl. '47. Bosses are bunk. F. H. LaGuardia.

Atlantic Monthly. 188:45-6. S. '51. Bullying the civil service. T. W. Arnold.

Business Week. p 152. Mr. 24, '51. Obedience to the unenforceable.

Cambridge Journal. 3:259-76. F. '50. The present day state of ethics. H. D. Lewis.

Catholic World. 158:12-17. O. '43. Realism for tomorrow's politician. W. J. Blyton.

Catholic World. 158:496-7. F. '44. Thread that binds; interconnection between morality and politics. Gerhard Leibholz.

Catholic World. 159:385-90. Ag. '44. Political falsehood. J. M. Gillis.

*Catholic World. 173:346-51. Ag. '51. Civil rights and political integrity. G. C. Zahn.

Catholic World. 174:81-5. N. '51. Dare we criticize our leaders? J. B. Sheerin.

Christian Century. 60:737-9. Je. 23, '43. Can nations act morally? L. J. Shafer.

Christian Century. 61:1094-5. S. 27, '44. Democracy with a sneer.

Discussion. 61:1202-3. O. 18, '44.

Christian Century. 62:140-1. Ja. 31, '45. Our political immorality. R. H. Markham.

Christian Century. 62:172-3. F. 7, '45. Mr. Wallace's pay-off. O. G. Villard.

Christian Century. 62:326-7. Mr. 14, '45. Mr. Wallace's opportunity.

Christian Century. 67:553-4. My. 3, '50. Moral law in a reeling world. H. R. Luce.

Discussion. 67:649-50. My. 24, '50.

*Christian Century. 68:910-11. Ag. 8, '51. Congress against sin; editorial.

Christian Century. 68:1182-4. O. 17, '51. Deeper corruption.

Christian Century. 68:1245-7. O. 31, '51. Everybody is cheating.

Christian Century. 68:1363. N. 28, '51. Hierarchy asks rebirth of political morality.

Collier's. 113:14+. Mr. 25, '44. Hannegan-in again! George Creel.

Collier's. 122:14-15+. Ag. 7, '48. Philadelphia: corrupt and not contented. Dickson Hartwell.

Collier's. 126:18-19+. S. 30, '50. Capone gang muscles into big-time politics. Lester Velie.

Collier's. 127:90. Ap. 21, '51. White House carnival.

Collier's. 127:13-15+. Je. 9, '51. Something is rotten in the state of Texas. Gordon Schendel.

Collier's. 128:16-17+. S. 8, '51. Terror in Tennessee. Bill Davidson and Harold Twitty.

Commonweal. 38:625. O. 15, '43. Mr. Aurelio. C. G. Paulding.

Commonweal. 46:227. Je. 20, '47. In the very heart of America.

Commonweal. 50:502-4. S. 2, '49. Virginia picks a governor. L. T. King.

Commonweal. 54:445. Ag. 17, '51. Cadets and campaigners; Butler campaign.

Commonweal. 54:619-20. O. 5, '51. Young: a lost generation? Francis Downing.

Commonweal. 55:87-8. N. 2, '51. Fighting corruption. E. S. Skillin.

Commonweal. 55:187. N. 30, '51. Fruits of secularism.

Contemporary Review. 176:181-5. S. '49. Bedrock; suppression and distortion of the truth. George Glasgow.

Contemporary Review. 176:306-10. N. '49. Quicksands. George Glasgow.

Current History. 7:374-9. N. '44. How good are campaign promises? D. G. Redmond.

*Guaranty Survey. 41:1-4. N. '51. Economics and morals.

Ladies' Home Journal. 65:53+. S. '48. Will they count your vote? Thomas Sweeney.

*Ladies' Home Journal. 68:11+. O. '51. Democracy in theory and practice. Dorothy Thompson.
*Ladies' Home Journal. 68:47. O. '51. Who cares? editorial.
*Ladies' Home Journal. 68:51+. O. '51. What women did in Gary.
Ladies' Home Journal. 68:53. N. '51. Boys in the back room.
*Ladies' Home Journal. 69:48. Ja. '52. To make your vote count. Margaret Hickey.
*Ladies' Home Journal. 69:48+. Ja. '52. It's time women took direct action. E. D. Canham.
Nation. 137:229. Ag. 30. '33. Politics and crime; editorial.
Nation. 159:289-91. S. 9, '44. Pennsylvania's G. O. P. is worried.
Nation. 167:9-10. Jl. 3, '48. Corrupt and discontented. I. K. Fagan.
Nation. 169:170-2. Ag. 20, '49. Big fix in Los Angeles. Carey McWilliams.
*Nation. 173:45-8. Jl. 21, '51. Pressure to buy and corrupt. H. H. Wilson.
Nation. 173:438-41. N. 24, '51. Cynics and feeble good men. H. H. Wilson.
National Municipal Review. 38:546-50+. D. '49. Who gets the billion graft? D. D. McKean.
Nation's Business. 39:17-18. Ag. '51. State of the nation; Fulbright Resolution. Felix Morley.
Nation's Business. 39:19-20. N. 51. State of the nation; bribery and corruption. Felix Morley.
New Republic. 107:268. S. 7, '42. How Pappy got in.
New Republic. 109:683-4. N. 15, '43. Aurelio affair. Justitia, pseud.
New Republic. 110:144-6. Ja. 31, '44. Hague is the law. W. L. Wiener.
New Republic. 110:625-7. My. 8, '44. Pew of Pennsylvania. Potomacus, pseud.
New Republic. 111:824. D. 18, '44. Graft in Albany.

New Republic. 123:17. Jl. 10, '50. War in Korea. H. L. Ickes.

*New Republic. 123:11-13. S. 11, '50. Dirty money and dirty politics. Louise Overacker.

New Republic. 123:13-14. O. 30, '50. Corrupt, callous, and contented. Mickey Levine.

New Republic. 124:25. F. 26, '51. Army engineers are too generous. H. L. Ickes.

New Republic. 124:5-6. Mr. 26, '51. Truman is to blame.

New Republic. 124:14-16. Ap. 2, '51. Political Murder, Inc. Helen Fuller.

New Republic. 124:15-16. Ap. 9, '51. Million dollar senators. J. Begeman.

New Republic. 125:8. Jl. 2, '51. Clean-up campaigns; bill curbing costs of political campaigns.

New Republic. 125:8. Ag. 13, '51. Maryland's folly.

New Republic. 125:7. O. 8, '51. Outside income.

New Republic. 125:7. O. 29, '51. Who steals the common. . . .

*New York Times. p 12. S. 28, '51. Truman's message to Congress.

*New York Times. p E1. D. 9, '51. Tax scandals; an issue for '52.

New York Times Magazine. p 14-15+. Je. 4, '44. How to get rid of the bosses. Charles Edison.

New York Times Magazine. p20+. Ap. 11, '48. It costs too much to run for office. R. L. Neuberger.

*New York Times Magazine. p 12+. Ap. 1, '51. We need a new code in Washington. Paul H. Douglas.

Same abr. with title We need a code of official conduct. Reader's Digest. 58:4-6. Je. '51.

New York Times Magazine. p 12+. Ap. 29, '51. Acid test for our character. H. S. Commager.

*New York Times Magazine. p 10+. O. 28, '51. Big danger is apathy to corruption. D. L. Cohn.

Newsweek. 22:46. D. 27, '43. Dewey rides again; charges against the O'Connell machine.

Newsweek. 24:31-3. N. 20, '44. Little Tammany; Albany investigation.
Newsweek. 37:38+. Ap. 23, '51. Scandal in Mississippi.
Newsweek. 38:24. Ag. 13, '51. Challenge to Congress; Tydings-Butler campaign. E. K. Lindley.
Newsweek. 38:24. O. 29, '51. Study in public morals.
Parliamentary Affairs. 3:187-96. Winter '49. Politicians, parties, and pressure groups. T. V. Smith.
Reader's Digest. 56:7-11. Je. '50. Twilight of honor. Fulton Oursler.
Reader's Digest. 57:153-6. N. '50. Dangerous decline of political morality. R. A. Taft.
Rotarian. 65:26-8. N. '44. Do you wink at it? V. W. Peterson.
Saturday Evening Post. 222:12. Mr. 4, '50. Officials in the people's democracies are more corrupt than reactionaries. Paul Vajda.
Saturday Evening Post. 223:34+. Ja. 27, '51. We gave 'em fits in Colorado. E. M. Hunter.
Saturday Evening Post. 224:17-19+. Ag. 11, '51. Case of Millville, N.J. S. B. Frank.
Senior Scholastic. 54:15-16. My. 18, '49. Right and wrong; how can we build a personal moral and ethical code? P. A. Knowlton.
Senior Scholastic. 59:16. O. 31, '51. To do what's right.
Time. 44:18. D. 18, '44. Lu-lu system.
Time. 56:13. Jl. 3, '50. Rice pudding with raisins in Jersey City.
Time. 57:30. Ap. 23, '51. Jobs for a price in Mississippi.
Time. 58:22-6. O. 8, '51. Boyle's Law.
Time. 58:24. O. 8, '51. It's not done in Britain: public morality. D. Richardson.
Time. 58:21-4. O. 22, '51. Congress: weighed in the balance.
United States News & World Report. 28:11-13. Ap. 21, '50. Politics hides gambling rackets.

United States News & World Report. 28:60. Ap. 21, '50. Letter from a housewife who calls for a new spirit. E. W. McKay.

United States News & World Report. 28:16-17. My. 12, '50. Crime's grip on politics: racketeering.

*United States News & World Report. 29:56. N. 3, '50. Politics, good and bad. David Lawrence.

United States News & World Report. 30:15-17. Mr. 30, '51. Crime, politics: national link; Senate crime investigation.

United States News & World Report. 31:17. Jl. 20, '51. Cocktail party morals; behavior in Washington.

United States News & World Report. 31:39-40. Ag. 10, '51. Ethics and public morals: the problem facing government; letter to Paul Douglas. Charles Sawyer.

United States News & World Report. 31:80. S. 28, '51. Left wing unmorality. David Lawrence.

United States News & World Report. 31:24-33. O. 26, '51. Ethics in government; interview. H. H. Vaughan.

Vital Speeches of the Day. 10:652-5. Ag. 15, '44. Party vs. personal government. R. C. Moley.

Vital Speeches of the Day. 11:156-8. D. 15, '44. Morality of public servants. G. E. Stringfellow.

Vital Speeches of the Day. 15:632-4. Ag. 1, '49. Aggressive citizenship. E. A. Johnston.

Vital Speeches of the Day. 16:66-8. N. 15, '49. What kind of government ahead? D. D. Eisenhower.

Vital Speeches of the Day. 17:17-20. O. 15, '50. For this we fight. G. N. Craig.

Vital Speeches of the Day. 17:45-7. N. 1, '50. Peace of truth. G. E. Sokolsky.

*Vital Speeches of the Day. 17:386-7. Ap. 15, '51. Moral standards of governmental conduct. J. W. Fulbright.

Vital Speeches of the Day. 17:645-9. Ag. 15, '51. Rededication to Pilgrim ideals. R. A. Taft.

*Vital Speeches of the Day. 17:716-18. S. 15, '51. Concerning honor in public life. Herbert Hoover.

Vital Speeches of the Day. 18:75-7. N. 15, '51. Ethics of organized influence. W. S. Symington.
Vital Speeches of the Day. 18:77-80. N. 15, '51. Teacher and political morality. G. P. Rice, Jr.
*Vital Speeches of the Day. 18:80-2. N. 15, '51. Morality in public life. Alistair Cooke.
*Yale Review. 40, no4:577-91. [Je.] '51. Ethics in public life. August Heckscher.

10382